CONTENTS

Using This Book 1

[1] Wassup Japanese 6

[2] Hang Out Japanese 25

[3] Hungry Japanese 39

[4] Flirting Japanese 53

[5] Couple Japanese 75

[6] Body Japanese 86

[7] Horny Japanese 103

[8] Sexy Onomatopoeia 138

[9] Angry Japanese 146

[10] LGBTQIA+ Japanese 159

Postscript 167

Acknowledgments 170

About the Author 171

USING THIS BOOK

Welcome to *Dirty Japanese, Second Edition*! This version builds on the original, updating the vocabulary to modern, commonly used Japanese words and phrases.

First, regarding vocabulary: If you are learning Japanese, you may have experienced someone saying, "No one uses that word," or you may wonder, "Do I sound natural, or do I sound like a textbook?" In this book, only words and phrases that Japanese people use today in Japan have been included. I have applied a star system (★) to show how much a word or phrase is typically used. If it is spoken often, there are three stars (★★★); if it is spoken infrequently, there is one star (★). Why is this update to more natural phrases important? Imagine that you met the love of your life in Japan, and just as you were about to get intimate, you turned to them and said, 差し込んでいい? (*Sashikonde ii?*: "Can I plug in?"). The sweet atmosphere would be broken, they might laugh, and the magic of the moment would disappear. How tragic! If you read this book, you would know to say, 入れてもいい? (*Iretemo ii?*: "Can I put it in?") instead, which sounds much more natural. Learning these nuances isn't something taught in textbooks or schools; that's what this book is here to help with.

Additionally, the book's structure and approach of introducing content has been improved. In *Dirty Japanese, Second Edition*, words and phrases are presented in a more interesting and memorable way. In medical school, I learned that the human brain can only retain what it either finds necessary for survival or fun and interesting. I've applied this simple concept to my own language learning, and with it I have mastered two languages besides my native Japanese. If you played video games as a kid, consider how many things you memorized. Complex button controls? Hundreds of monster names? But it was so much fun, you didn't even notice you were memorizing at the time, right? This book seeks to replicate that feeling.

Finally, I'll close by saying I believe this subject matter is important and, unfortunately, often shied away from. It's not included in textbooks, and not taught by teachers. If you asked a friend, "Teach me what you say during sex!" it might be a very awkward conversation. But these phrases are actually quite impactful, especially if you were to develop a close relationship with a Japanese speaker. I worked hard to make this the best source of "dirty Japanese" that exists. Even though I am a native speaker, I went so far as to confirm phrases with family, friends, and coworkers. I endured uncomfortable looks, and some people might have even changed the way they think about me. But it was a sacrifice in the pursuit of preparing readers like you for your future! I hope you enjoy this book and live a fun, fulfilling dirty life!

•••••Reading Japanese

If you haven't tackled the challenge of learning to read Japanese yet, it's not as hard as you might think. Japanese writing uses four different sets of characters.

Hiragana, full of loops and curves, is an "alphabet" made up of 46 characters representing every sound in the Japanese language—a, i, u, e, o, ka, ki, ku, ke, ko, sa, shi, su, se, so, ta, chi, tsu . . . and so on. It is usually used for writing basic Japanese words. The following words are written in hiragana:

おっす	*ossu*	what's up
いそぎんちゃく	*isoginchaku*	sea anemone

Katakana, a simple, angular "alphabet," also has 46 characters. Each one corresponds to a hiragana character, though there can be subtle differences in pronunciation that you don't really need to worry about. It is usually used for writing borrowed foreign words (like "computer"), foreign names, company names, and newly coined Japanese words (like "karaoke"). Here are some examples of katakana:

トム・クルーズ	*tomu kurūzu*	Tom Cruise
コンピューター	*konpyūtā*	computer
ラーメン	*rāmen*	ramen

Kanji, which looks very complicated, is a set of "ideograms" imported from China as early as the 5th century. Each character represents an idea or a full word and can be grouped in different combinations to create more complex words. There are thousands of kanji characters, and many of them have multiple different readings and pronunciations depending on the context and combination they're used in. So good luck with that. . . Fortunately, teachers say you only need to know 1,945 kanji characters for complete Japanese literacy. Most of the others are only used to represent the names of specific places and people, so you can think of them as corporate logos and only learn to recognize the ones you need. For example:

女子高生	*joshi kōsei*	schoolgirl
美人薄命	*bijin hakumei*	beautiful women, bad fates
喧嘩上等	*kenka jōtō*	tough motherfucker

Romaji, the Roman (English) alphabet, is now spreading to Japan because of globalization. You'll encounter it in Japanese slang, especially for writing abbreviations and acronyms of American words and high-tech terms.

You'll find complete lists of hiragana and katakana characters, along with the basic kanji characters, in the front or back of most standard Japanese–English phrasebooks. Study them and challenge yourself to relate them to the words and phrases in this book. I hereby promise that anybody can learn to read hiragana and katakana in about a week, if sufficiently motivated.

•••••Pronouncing Japanese

Japanese grammar may be mind-boggling, but at least the words are easy to pronounce. Once your tongue gets used to the basic syllables, you should be able to read out loud from this or any other phrasebook well enough for local people to understand you.

Japanese has the same five vowels as English, and almost all words end with a vowel or an "n." Each vowel has only one pronunciation:

a = short "a" as in "father"
i = "ee" as in "keep"
u = "oo" as in "loop"
e = short "e" as in "get"
o = regular "o" as in "Oh baby, oh baby, oh baby!"

Sometimes, when reading Japanese words written in the Roman alphabet, you'll see a vowel with a straight line above it, like "ā" or "ō." This means the vowel is drawn out longer. So "ō" means "Ohhh . . . ," not "Oooo . . ." Additionally, there are no strict rules defining exactly how to use spaces when writing using romaji.

Consonant sounds in Japanese are pretty much the same as in English, but there are fewer of them. The consonants that Americans tend to have trouble with are:

ts = like an "s" beginning with a little tongue click, similar but less pronounced than "itsy-bitsy" in English.

n = drawn out slightly longer than an English "n," like "Nnno . . . I don't think so."

r = rolled, similar to Spanish, but with only a single roll/flick of the tongue.

Even if you botch the pronunciation of these letters, people will still be able to understand you.

The most important point to remember is that every syllable in a Japanese word gets equal emphasis. It's "ka-wa-sa-ki," not "KA-wa-SA-ki."

CHAPTER 1

WASSUP JAPANESE

OSSU NIHONGO

おっす日本語

Welcome to the first chapter! Regardless of whether you are Japanese or not, first impressions almost always determine how the rest of a relationship unfolds. So, let us begin with some basic greetings.

Japanese people use polite language with new acquaintances (or in formal settings) and casual language with friends. Since polite language is already taught in textbooks, this book will focus on casual language.

This book will cover as much content as possible through examples, helping you learn Japanese vocabulary and contemporary culture along the way.

So let's take a quick look!

Greetings are the most important factor in building trust between people. For this reason, it's important to remember the greetings that appear here.

••••• Hello

konnichiwa

こんにちは

Japanese slang isn't really used when talking to strangers, so there aren't a lot of meet-and-greet types of slang words. If you're being introduced to somebody for the very first time, you gotta settle for a good old-fashioned *konnichiwa*.

Hello ★★★
konnichiwa
こんにちは

Hello / Thank you ★★
dōmo
どうも
The phrase *dōmo* is sometimes used as a greeting, and sometimes as a word of thanks, as well as in a wide range of other ambiguous situations.

••••• What's up?

ossu

おっす

Ossu is a slangier way of saying "hello." It is especially used when you run into someone close to you, like a friend. Although it is more often used by men, it is not strange for women to use it. Like its English counterpart "what's up," *ossu* has an infinite number of variations. *Ossu* was originally an incredibly formal word, the kind of thing that a soldier would say to a drill sergeant—like: "SIR, YES, SIR!" But in a slang context, *ossu* comes across as a casual way to say "hi."

Almost everything written below has the same meaning, with minor nuanced differences. Rather than learning the very minor differences, it is best to learn them in order of frequency of use. Make sure to memorize the ones with ★★★, which are used most commonly.

What's up! (greeting) ★★★
ossu
おっす！

What's up! (variant) ★★
oissu
おいっす！

Sup! ★★★
yo
よっ!

Sup! How are you doing? ★★★
yo! genki?
よっ!元気?

Sup ★★
ussu
うっす
Mainly a response, sometimes a greeting.

Whazzap! ★★
uissu
ういっす！
Mainly a greeting, sometimes a response.

Roger (only a response) ★★
ui
うい

Hello (casual) ★★
konchiwa
こんちは
This comes from *konnichiwa*.

Hi ★★★
yahho
やっほ

Hey ★
ya
やっ

•••••Good morning / Good evening
ohayō / konbanwa
おはよう・こんばんは

There are also informal variations on "good morning" and "good evening":

G'morning! ★★★
ohayō
おはよ
I have the feeling that more people use *ohayō* when sending messages nowadays.

Good morning, Sunshine! ★★
ohhā
おっはー
This presents as slightly *gyaru*. (See page 59 for a description of the Japanese *gyaru* personality type.)

I don't think there is a casual way of saying "good evening." A lot of people say things like *ussu*, or *yahho*.

As in English, the next part of a greeting usually involves inquiring about the other person's well-being.

Long time no see. ★★★
hisashiburi
ひさしぶり。

Long time no see! (more casual) ★★
ohisa
おひさ!

How's it hangin'? ★★★
chōshi dou
調子どう?

Same as always. ★★★
ai kawarazu dayo
相変わらずだよ。

Yo! ★★★
yo
よっ!

It's been a while. ★★
hisa bisa dane
久々だね。

Same old bullshit. ★
dōmokōmo nēyo
どうもこうもねーよ。

••••••Goodbye
sayōnara
さようなら

Sayōnara is used as a goodbye. In Japanese, it is widely used as a general way of saying "goodbye," but it is also a formal phrase, and I get the impression it is not actually used much at all.

Some people say it means a permanent farewell, but that's not necessarily the case. Even in elementary school, when leaving, everyone says *sayōnara!* However, it is certainly also used when saying farewell forever, so the meaning changes depending on the context, facial expression, and way of saying it.

Goodbye ★★
sayōnara
さようなら
When it comes to parting phrases, there are also any number of variations on the traditional *sayōnara*.

Goodbye (more casual) ★★★
sayonara
さよなら

Goodbye (more old-fashioned) ★
sainara
さいなら

Buh-bye ★
bainara
ばいなら

See ya ★★★
jā ne
じゃあね

Later ★★★
mata ne
またね

Smell you later ★
aba yo
あばよ
Tough-guy way of saying "bye."

……Sorry
gomennasai
ごめんなさい

It is said Japanese people often apologize, and I agree. However, sometimes it's not an apology for their actions; they're apologizing to show respect to the other person. If I know someone is angry with me, I will say *sumimasen* (excuse me) regardless of whether or not I am at fault. I will not use *gomen nasai* (I'm sorry), because that has a stronger meaning as an apology. By using *sumimasen*, you are showing you respect the person who is angry with you, and you can start talking from there. People are emotional creatures, so whether or not you say the word *sumimasen* in Japan can make a big difference to the situation that follows.

I'm sorry ★★★
gomen nasai
ごめんなさい

I'm sorry ★
gomenchai
ごめんちゃい
A little old-fashioned way of saying it.

Ex-squeeze me ★
gomenkusai
ごめんくさい

Whoopsy-daisy ★
mengo mengo
めんごめんご

Sorrusy* ★
sumanko
すまんこ

*This is a play on words. The word *manko* means "pussy."

Excuse me / Sorry ★★★
sumimasen
すみません

"Excuse me" is one of those multipurpose phrases in English; it can be a greeting, a good-bye, or an apology for, say, farting. The same goes for Japanese—you can use these slang variations of "excuse me" in a variety of situations.

Pardon (a little more casual) ★★
suimasen
すいません

Well, pardon me for living! ★★
ikitete suimasen
生きてすいません!

'Scuse me (very casual) ★★
suman
すまん

'Scuse my shitty Japanese. ★★
nihongo ga hetakuso de suman
日本語がへたくそですまん。

I apologize sincerely (very formal) ★★★
moshiwake arimasen
申し訳ありません

My bad (a little tacky) ★
warīne
わりぃーね

SORRY (EXTREMELY)

DOGEZA
土下座

Have you ever heard of the term *dogeza*? When Japanese people really want to apologize from the bottom of their hearts, they have a special way of apologizing, as shown in the picture. This is called *dogeza*. While I myself have never seen anyone actually do this in person, this is not just a figment of our imagination, and it is still done in real life. For example, when a celebrity does something wrong and holds a press conference, there is a chance that you might see it. Or, if you have an affair just before getting married, you might end up on your knees apologizing to your partner's parents.

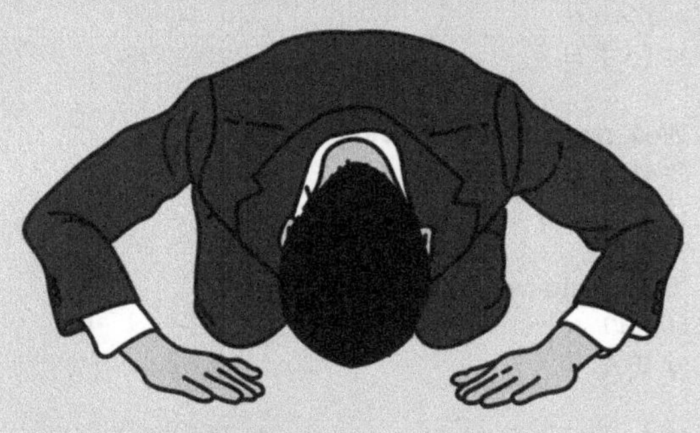

••••••Myself

jibun
自分

One of the great things about Japanese is the variety of personal pronouns you can assume.

I (feminine/polite) ★★★
watashi
私
Watashi is the most common first-person pronoun in Japanese. It is used widely in both everyday conversation and formal situations, regardless of gender, age, or social status. It shows politeness and respect toward others.

I'm Hiyori (name).
watashi *wa hiyori desu*
私は日和です。

I (boyish) ★★★
boku
僕
Boku is a first-person pronoun that gives a more casual and masculine impression. Generally used by men to refer to themselves. Often seen in situations where male friendship and familiarity are felt.

I'm studying as hard as I can to get into college!
boku *wa isshō kenmei juken benkyō o yatte imasu*
僕は一生懸命受験勉強をやっています!

I (masculine) ★★★
ore
俺
Ore is a more casual and manly first-person pronoun. Generally used by men to assert themselves strongly. It is mostly used among close friends and family.

I totally look like Hitoki from Onomappu, don't I?
ore *tte Onomappu no Hitoki ni nitenne*
俺って、Onomappuのひときに似てね?
Hitoki is the author and Onomappu is his YouTube channel.

Hitoki is the name of this book's author. If you've forgotten, get a tattoo of my name on your butt.
Hitoki wa kono chosha no namae desu. Moshi kimi ga sore o wasurete itara, o shiri ni boku no namae no tattoo o irete ne
ひときはこの著者の名前です。もし君がそれを

忘れていたら、お尻に僕の名前のタトゥーを入れてね。

I (female, girl) ★
uchi
うち

Uchi is a first-person pronoun used mainly in Western Japanese dialects, but it can also be heard in parts of Eastern Japan. It is generally used by women to refer to themselves. However, in the Kanto (Eastern Japan) region at least, it can give the impression of being a little immature.

I don't want to go to school today.
uchi, *kyo gakko ikitakunai wa*
うち、今日学校いきたくないわ。

I (very formal) ★★
watakushi
わたくし

Watakushi is a more formal and polite first-person pronoun. It is used for self-introductions and statements in formal or business situations. It is used in situations where you want to be modest about making your own point, or to show special respect to the other person.

I (Female, a little girl.) ★★
atashi
あたし

Atashi is a more informal pronoun and is used mainly by women. It is less commonly used today because it gives the impression of being a bit provincial.

Are you coming to my place tonight?
konya ***atashi no*** *ie kuru*
今夜あたしの家来る?

·····Introducing others

tako shokai

他己紹介

Let's introduce your new friend! In Japanese, there are several different pronouns you can use to refer to other people.

Small talk

Takeshi: Hello everyone. Today I'm going to introduce you all to my new friend!
Takeshi: minna konnichiwa. kyo wa atarashii tomodachi o shokai suru yo!
たけしこんにちは。今日は新しい友達を紹介するよ!

His name is Hitoki!
koitsu no namae wa hitoki da yo
こいつの名前は ひとき だよ!

He's a real-life virgin!
kare wa honmono no dōtei da yo
彼は本物の童貞だよ!

Hitoki: H . . . Hi, everyone. (You fucker . . . Don't be ridiculous . . . You're the one who's a virgin ...)
Hitoki: ya . . . yaa, minna (te me . . . fu zakennayo . . . omae koso dōtei darou ga . . .)
ひとき: や...やあ、みんな(てめぇ...ふざけんなよ...お前こそ童貞だろうが...)

By the way, there is an interesting rumor in Japan. The legend differs depending on the region, but if you remain a virgin until a certain age, you get a special title:

30-year-old virgin ★★★
mahou tsukai
魔法使い
Literally, "wizard."

40-year-old virgin ★★
yousei
妖精
Literally, "fairy."

45-year-old virgin ★
tenkuu bito
天空人
Literally, "celestial being."

50-year-old virgin ★
ningen kokuhou
人間国宝
Literally, "living national treasure."

55-year-old virgin ★
kami
神
Literally, "god, who can even control nature."

60-year-old virgin ★
furou fushi
不老不死
Literally, "being who can achieve immortality."

In particular, it is well known that if you are a virgin until the age of 30, you can become a wizard.

Leaving that aside, let's get straight to studying our main theme!

You (polite) ★★★
anata
あなた
Anata is a generic second-person pronoun, used to refer to someone in a polite or neutral manner. It can lack intimacy compared to other pronouns.

Wait, could it be that you are Hitoki?
*e, moshikashite **anata** wa hitoki desu ka*
え、もしかして**あなた**はひときですか？

TITLES

KEISHŌ

敬称

If you have studied Japanese even a little, you may have seen the suffix *san* after names. In fact, there are various other ways of addressing people's names, and all of them are only used as suffixes. In addition to honorifics, there are also colloquial ways of addressing friends.

San... ★★★
さん
Pretty much the equivalent of "Mister," it maintains professional distance.

Sama... ★★★
さま
"Sir/Madam." Only for highly polite situations, or when you're being sarcastic.

Kun... ★★★
くん
An affectionate ending for a friend's name, usually a male friend who is the same age or younger than you.

Chan... ★★★
ちゃん
More affectionate and cuter that *kun*, and therefore often used with girls, but with boys as well, when they are being cute.

Tan... ★
たん
An even slangier version of *chan*.

Sensei... ★★★
先生
Sensei is generally used for teachers, doctors, or someone who has otherwise been a beacon of knowledge in one's life.

You (casual) ★★★
omae
お前
Omae is a second-person pronoun that is often used among equals, friends, or in casual situations. However, depending on

the tone or context, it can have a negative connotation. In general, it can be more assertive and less polite than *anata*.

I like you.
*ore wa **omae** ga suki da*
俺はお前が好きだ。

He/She/It ★★★
koitsu
こいつ
Koitsu is a colloquial word used to refer to people, things, and sometimes even animals in a casual setting; it can be slightly derogatory. It is a colloquial expression, and depending on the tone and context, it can either indicate familiarity or contempt. It is often used between friends or in a relaxed environment.

I hate him.
*ore wa **koitsu** ga kirai da*
俺はこいつが嫌いだ。

You (casually polite) ★★★
kimi
君
Kimi is a second-person pronoun that is generally used in casual situations and in close relationships, especially between friends and in romantic relationships. It indicates intimacy and familiarity, but in certain situations it may be overly familiar or give an informal impression.

What's your name?
***kimi no** namae wa nani*
君の名前は何？

You fucker ★★
temē
てめぇ
Temē is a highly offensive second-person pronoun with negative or aggressive connotations. When used inappropriately, it is considered rude and disrespectful. It is mainly used in heated arguments, confrontations, or among close friends.

You fucker, don't be ridiculous!
***temē**, fuzakeru n janē zo*
てめぇ、ふざけるんじゃねーぞ!

You asshole ★
kisama
貴様
Kisama is a very offensive and insulting word, used with the intention of showing contempt for the other person. It was originally a word of respect but is now regarded as a very rude word, used in situations where you want to insult the other person, or express anger or hostility. Depending on the situation and the relationship with the other person, it may be considered extremely inappropriate and objectionable. To be honest, its use is old-fashioned, and I myself have never heard it spoken. It is sometimes used in anime, historical dramas, and TV dramas.

You asshole, what the fuck are you doing there!
***kisama**, sokode nani o shite iru*
貴様, そこで何をしている!

••••••Friends
tomodachi
友達

Japan is often seen as a rigid society, where social pressures deny people their full range of expression. This is not true. What is acceptable to say depends on who's around. When you're with friends, you can say some of the stupidest stuff possible and still be loved and forgiven. But even with friends there are different levels of intimacy.

Friend ★★★
tomodachi
友達

Total stranger ★★★
aka no tanin
赤の他人

Hey—Japanese people don't just go up and talk to total strangers like that.
*anone nihonjin wa sōyatte **aka no tanin** ni koe o kaketari shinai no*
あのね、日本人はそうやって**赤の他人**に声をかけたりしないの。

Acquaintance ★★★
shiriai
知り合い

I first got interested in Japan because I had lots of Japanese acquaintances.
*nihon ni kyōmi o motta no wa nihonjin no **shiriai** ga ōkatta kara nanda*
日本に興味を持ったのは、日本人の**知り合い**が多かったからなんだ。

Classmate ★★★
dōkyūsei
同級生

Do you hang out with your classmates much?
***dōkyūsei** to wa yoku asondeiru no*
同級生とはよく遊んでいるの？

Coworker ★★★
dōryō
同僚

Have you ever dated a coworker?
***dōryō** to tsukiatta koto aru*
同僚と付き合ったことある？

Buddy-buddy ★★★
nakayoshi
仲良し

You know, we really get along well.
*uchiratte kekkō **nakayoshi** da ne*
うちらってけっこう**仲良し**だね。

Solid guy ★★★
ī yatsu
いいヤツ

He's really a solid guy.
aitsu wa hontō ni ***ī yatsu*** *da*
あいつは本当にいいヤツだ。

Sweet girl ★★★
ī ko
いい子

She's really a sweet girl.
kanojo wa hontō ni ***ī ko*** *de ne*
彼女は本当にいい子だね。

Email friend ★
merutomo
メルトモ
We don't use email much anymore, so this is an old word.

Best friend ★★★
shin'yū
親友

My best friend is Japanese.
shin'yū *wa nihonjin da*
親友は日本人だ。

Childhood friend ★★★
osana najimi
幼なじみだ

We are childhood friends.
koitsu to wa ***osana najimi*** *da*
こいつとは幼なじみだ。

Crush ★★★
sukina hito
好きな人

I think he's got a new crush.
*aitsu wa **sukina hito** ga dekita mitai*
あいつは好きな人ができたみたい。

Boyfriend ★★★
kareshi
彼氏

Your boyfriend seems like a really nice guy.
*kimi no **kareshi** wa yasashisō dane*
君の彼氏は優しそうだね。

Girlfriend ★★★
kanojo
彼女

Ex-girlfriend ★★★
moto kano
元カノ

My girl ★
yome
ヨメ

I'll introduce you to my girl sometime.
***yome** wa kondo shōkai suruyo*
ヨメは今度紹介するよ。

Friends with benefits ★★★
sefure
セフレ
This comes from "sex friend" セックスフレンド *(sekkusufurendo)*.

Is it wrong to have friends with benefits?
***Sefure** o tsukuru koto wa warui koto desu ka*
セフレを作ることは悪いことですか?

CHAPTER 2

HANG OUT JAPANESE

ODEKAKE NIHONGO

おでかけ日本語

You will probably make many Japanese friends in the future as you continue to study Japanese. In Japan, there are many occasions when we often go shopping with friends, go to game centers, or play sports. In this chapter, I will explain words related to these activities.

••••••Shopping

kaimono

買い物

What's this? ★★★

kore wa nan desu ka

これは何ですか?

That's good! ★★★

ii desu ne

いいですね!

I want this. ★★★
kore kudasai
これください。

How much is this? ★★★
kore wa ikura desu ka
これはいくらですか？

It's expensive. ★★★
takai desu
高いです。

It's too expensive! ★★★
takasugi desu
高すぎです！

It's cheap. ★★★
yasui desu
安いです。

Where is the cashier? ★★★
reji wa doko desu ka
レジはどこですか？

Where's my wallet? ★★
watashi no saifu wa doko desu ka
私の財布はどこですか？

I don't have money. ★★★
okane ga arimasen
お金がありません。

I don't need a plastic bag. ★★★
rejibukuro wa irimasen
レジ袋はいりません。

Do you need a receipt? ★★★
resīto wa irimasu ka
レシートはいりますか？

Do you want me to carry your baggage? ★★
kimi no baggu motou ka
君のバッグ持とうか?

Do you use a shopping cart? ★★
shoppingu kāto wa tsukau
ショッピングカートは使う?

I've spent too much money, I need to save. ★★
okane tsukaisugita kara setsuyaku suru hitsuyou ga aru na
お金使いすぎたから、節約する必要があるな。

In Kansai (western part of Japan), Kansai dialect is used, which is slightly different from standard Japanese, and you may hear the following words.

How much is this? (in Kansai dialect) ★★★
kore nanbo desu ka
これなんぼですか?

This is cute! (in Kansai dialect) ★★★
kore kawaee na
これかわええな!

Are you serious? (in Kansai dialect) ★★★
honma kai na
ほんまかいな?

·····Sports
supōtsu
スポーツ

In Japan, sports are a common topic of conversation, and I often watch or play sports with friends. In Japan, interest in baseball is particularly strong, with everyone from the young to the elderly watching it. It is very interesting to note that not only professional baseball but also high school baseball is one of the main interests of Japanese people. High school students who have devoted their entire youth to baseball, practicing hard every day, show us a moving story with tears in the stadium every summer. Thanks to them, Japanese businessmen are able to work hard during the day knowing that they'll get to relax watching a great baseball game after they're done.

Do you play...? ★★★
. . . yatteiru
…やっている?

I want to play... ★★★
. . . yaritai
…やりたい。

Let's watch the ... game. ★★★
. . .no shiai miyō ze
…の試合見ようぜ。

Soccer ★★★
sakkā
サッカー

Baseball ★★★
yakyū
野球

Kickboxing ★★
kikku bokushingu
キックボクシング

Golf ★★★
gorufu
ゴルフ

Basketball ★★★
basuke
バスケ

Rugby ★★★
ragubī
ラグビー

Tennis ★★★
tenisu
テニス

American football ★★
amefuto
アメフト

Sumo ★★★
sumō
相撲
If you're in Japan, be sure to take the opportunity to watch a sumo match. It's incredible live, but even on TV it never fails to entertain.

Explain the rules of sumo to me.
sumō *no rūru o setsumei shite kudasai*
相撲のルールを説明してください。

What... do you like? ★★★
sukina ... wa
好きな…は?

Sports ★★★
supōtsu
スポーツ

Teams ★★★
chīmu
チーム

Players ★★★
senshu
選手

••••••Minor sports
mainā supōtsu
マイナースポーツ

Around the major entertainment hubs of Tokyo (Shinjuku, Shibuya, Ikebukuro, and so on), you'll find places to play all the world's minor sports—ping-pong, bowling, pool, darts, air hockey, and batting cages. If you ever miss the last train, contact a friend to play these sports together and have a fun night!

Wanna go play some... ★★★
yari ni ikō ka
…やりに行こうか?

Ping-pong ★★★
takkyū
卓球

Bowling ★★★
bōringu
ボーリング

Pool ★★
biriyādo
ビリヤード

Darts ★★★
dātsu
ダーツ

Air hockey ★★
eāhokkē
エアーホッケー

Batting cages ★★
battingu
バッティング

Mahjong ★
mājan
麻雀

••••• Cheering
ōen
応援

When a friend invites you to play sports with a group, you're expected to cheer them on and make them look good. If you pay more attention to your cell phone instead, they probably won't invite you to join again next time. So, for these times, you need to know how to cheer. Use the words here to get everyone going!

Go! ★★★
gambare
がんばれ!

Fight! ★★★
faito
ファイト!

Nice! ★★★
naisu
ナイス!

Hurray! ★
furē furē
フレーフレー!

Almost! ★★★
ato sukoshi
あと少し!

You can do it! ★★★
ikeru
いける!

Not yet! ★★
mada mada
まだまだ!

You did a great job! ★★★
ganbatta ne
頑張ったね!

••••••Exercise
undō
運動

It's hard to get motivated when you exercise solo. So find a workout buddy to hold you accountable. When you do, use these phrases.

Let's do...together! ★★★
isshoni…shiyou
一緒に...しよう!

Exercise ★★★
undō
運動

Practice ★★★
renshū
練習

Weight training ★★★
kintore
筋トレ

Jogging ★★★
jogingu
ジョギング

Yoga ★★★
yoga
ヨガ

Swimming ★★★
suiei
水泳

Stretching ★★★
sutoretchi
ストレッチ

I want to work out my... ★★★
... o kitaetainda
…を鍛えたいんだ。

Abs ★★★
fukkin
腹筋

Biceps ★★★
nitō kin
二頭筋

Triceps ★★
santō kin
三頭筋

Pecs ★★★
kyōkin
胸筋

Thighs ★★
futomomo
太もも

Calves ★★
fukurahagi
ふくらはぎ

Want to go to the gym? ★★★
jimu ni ikitai
ジムに行きたい?

Would you spot me? ★★
*chotto **hojo** shite moraemasu ka*
ちょっと**補助**してもらえますか?

I've started to sweat. ★★★
***ase** kaichatta*
汗かいちゃった。

I'm exhausted. ★★★
tsukareta
疲れた。

I'm out of breath. ★★★
***ikigire** shichatta*
息切れしちゃった。

I'm all sore today. ★★★
kyō wa kinnikutsū da
今日は筋肉痛だ。

•••••Arcade
gēmu sentā
ゲームセンター

Arcades are places where Japanese junior and senior high school students gather to take a break from boring school life. And since students from different schools go there too, arcades are also places where students can meet new friends and lovers. Many people, including myself, still remember that exciting feeling even after growing up, so adults sometimes go there to have fun too.

I like ... very much. ★★★
...ga totemo suki
…がとても好き。

Amusement arcade ★★ / **Amusement arcade** (more casual) ★★★
gēmu sentā / gēsen
ゲームセンター / ゲーセン

Crane game ★★★ / **Crane game** (variant) ★★
kurēn gēmu / yūfō kyacchā
クレーンゲーム / UFOキャッチャー

Photo sticker booths ★★★
purikura
プリクラ

Many Japanese women have had their picture taken with this machine at least once. They enter a small box-shaped machine, where they can take a cute, corrected photo. They can then doodle on the photo as they wish, and the printed photo can be affixed as a sticker. Although the boom has now passed, it is still immensely popular.

COIN PUSHER GAMES

MEDARU GĒMU

メダルゲーム

Coin Pusher games ★ / Coin Pusher games (variant) ★★★
medaru gēmu / koin gēmu
メダルゲーム / コインゲーム

This game is played by putting coin-like, metal tokens into a machine and then dropping in other tokens to get them. It works like a casino, but the metal tokens cannot be redeemed for cash. My foreign friend once asked me why people buy the tokens and play this game if they can't get money for it. I like this game too, but had never thought about this issue before. I believe people genuinely enjoy the game even though no money is involved.

•••••Video games

gēmu

ゲーム

Japanese-founded SONY and Nintendo are global leaders in gaming; the companies have brought excitement and enthusiasm to kids of all ages, offering a platform for users to make new friends and feel accepted in the world.

Do you have... ★★★
... motteru
…持ってる?

Wanna play some... ★★★
... yarō ka
…やろうか?

Are you good at... ★★★
... umai no
…うまいの?

I'm bad at ... ★★★
watashi ... heta dayo
私…下手だよ。

Playstation ★★★
puresute
プレステ

Nintendo Switch ★★★
nintendō suicchi
任天堂スイッチ

X-box ★
ekkusu bokkusu
Xボックス

Famicom ★
famikon
ファミコン
Nintendo's Famicom was the precursor to the NES you know today.

Pokémon ★★★
pokemon
ポケモン

Animal Crossing ★★★
dōbutsu no mori
どうぶつの森

Mario Cart ★★★
mario kāto
マリオカート

Monster Hunter ★★★
monhan
モンハン

Smash Bros ★★★
sumabura
スマブラ

Minecraft ★★★
maikura
マイクラ

Dragon Quest ★★★
dorakue
ドラクエ

Let's relax and play games at home today! ★★★
kyou wa ie de yukkuri ***gēmu*** *yarou yo*
今日は家でゆっくりゲームやろうよ!

I'm not a big gamer, but I like video games. ★★
gēmā made dewa nai kedo ***gēmu*** *suki dayo*
ゲーマーまでではないけど、ゲーム好きだよ。

Oh, isn't this game buggy? ★★★
e kono ***gēmu*** *bagu tte nai*
え、このゲームバグってない?

CHAPTER 3

HUNGRY JAPANESE

PEKO PEKO NIHONGO

ペコペコ日本語

Food is always popular everywhere. As you know, Japan has many popular foods such as sushi, takoyaki, sukiyaki, and tonkatsu. Let's learn some Japanese words related to food in this chapter and use them with your Japanese friends and loved ones!

I'll eat this. ★★★
itadakimasu
いただきます。

It was a great meal. ★★★
gochisousama
ごちそうさま。

Enjoy your meal! ★★
meshiagare
召し上がれ！

In Japanese, when you say, "I'm hungry," the subject is "お腹 (*onaka*: the belly)." Isn't that cute?

GRATITUDE AT MEALTIME

Let's eat.
Itadakimasu
いただきます.

Thank you for the food.
gochisōsama
ごちそうさま.

Itadakimasu and *gochisōsama* are said before and after a meal, respectively, but their true meanings cannot be translated. Both are words to express gratitude for all things related to the meal, including the ingredients used in the meal, the people who grew them, the people who carried them, and the people who cooked them, etc. We say it when we eat alone or with family and friends.

My belly is... ★★★
onaka ga...
お腹が…

Famished ★★★
hetta
へった

Starving ★★
peko peko da
ペコペコだ

Full ★★★
ippai
いっぱい

Stuffed ★★
pan pan
パンパン

Growling ★
goro goro itteru
ゴロゴロ言ってる

Hurting ★★★
itai
痛い

••••• Excuse me!
sumimasen
すみません!

すみません (*sumimasen*: excuse me) is a word we use really often in everyday life. It is said when ordering food, talking to the clerk at the supermarket, asking directions to a stranger, etc. It also means "I'm sorry," as it is used when you really want to apologize to someone.

Excuse me, but… ★★★
sumimasen ga. . .
すみませんが …

. . .can we order? ★★★
. . .chūmon shite mo ī desuka
…注文してもいいですか?

. . .what do you recommend? ★★★
. . .nanika osusume wa arimasu ka
…何かお薦めはありますか?

. .what's in this? ★★★
. . .kore wa nani ga haitteirundesu ka
…これは何が入っているんですか?

. . .can I get a menu? ★★★
. . .me'nyū o kudasai
…メニューをください?

. . .this tastes weird. ★
. . .kore aji ga hen desu
…これ、味が変です。

. . .can I get some water? ★★★
. . .mizu o kudasai
…水をください?

. . .can I get a fork? ★★★
. . .fōku o kudasai
…フォークをください。

. . .how much longer will it take? ★★★
. . .dore kurai kakarisou desu ka
…どれくらいかかりそうですか?

. . .can I have your phone number? ★★
. . .denwabangō o oshiete moraemasu ka
…電話番号を教えてもらえますか?

••••••Delicious

oishii

おいしい

From exploring what makes a good soy sauce, to the secret to making a delicious beef curry, to finding the best rāmen shops in Osaka—food culture has found its medium in Japanese television. And on these many food programs, every time the hosts taste something new, they inevitably make some comment about how delicious it is. The meaning of these comments basically boils down to "DELICIOUS!!!!" but they take on a number of forms, including the following:

This is good! (casual) ★★★
kore ***umai***
これうまい!

This is delicious! ★★★
kore ***oishī***
これおいしい!

Fantabulous! ★
geki uma
激ウマ!

Seriously, this is goooood. ★
majikayo kore umē
まじかよ、これうめぇー。

It melts in my mouth. ★
kuchi no naka de ***torokeru.***
口の中でとろける。

It smells amazingly good. ★
sugē ī *kaori*
すげーいい香り。

Can I get seconds? ★★★
okawari *moraemasu ka*
おかわりもらえますか?

You're eating too much! ★★★
omae tabesugi dayo
お前食べ過ぎだよ!

I'd like to talk to the chef. ★
shefu to hanashitai desu
シェフと話したいです。

I want to marry the cook. ★
tsukutta hito to ***kekkon*** *shitai*
作った人と結婚したい。

•••••Yuck

mazui
まずい

It's pretty hard to find food that is actually bad in Japan. Even the school lunches served at the most underfunded elementary schools in Japan are delicious. However, if the food is not to your liking, you might try saying something like this to your Japanese friends.

This tastes bad. ★★★
kore mazui ne
これまずいね。

This tastes a little weird. ★★★
aji ga chotto hen dayo
味がちょっと変だよ。

No, that's extremely gross. ★★
iya gekimazu da na
いや､激マズだな。

This is shit. ★★
kore kuso dayo
これクソだよ。

This is shit among shit. ★
kuso chuu no kuso dane
糞中の糞だね。

Seriously, this is poop. ★
unko da ne maji de
うんこだねマジで。

I can't eat this. ★★
konna mono kuenē
こんなもの食えねー。

This restaurant is really the worst. ★★★
kono mise wa majide saiaku
この店はまじで最悪。

••••• Food
tabemono
食べ物

Technically, *gohan* is the word for "rice." But of course, everybody knows that rice is popular all across Asia! So, in Asia, the word "rice" can be used interchangeably with "food."

Food ★★★
gohan
ご飯

Did you already eat…? ★★★
… tabeta
…食べた?

I want to EAT…!!! ★★
… kuitē
…食いてぇーーー!

I love… ★★★
… daisuki
…大好き。

What kind of… do you feel like? ★★★
… dō suru?
…どうする?

What's your favorite...? ★★★
ichiban sukina ... wa?
一番好きな…は?

Why don't I fix you some...? ★★★
... tsukutte ageyō ka
…作ってあげようか?

I want some cheap, greasy...! ★★
yasukute aburappoi ... ga kuitai
安くて油っぽい…が食いたい!

Wanna order some takeout...? ★★
... wa demae tanomō ka
…は出前頼もうか?

••••••Cuisine
ryouri
料理

One of the best things about Japan is that the food is really good. Of course, this is partly because I am Japanese, but so far I do not have any overseas friends who do not like Japanese food.

Let's get some... ★★★
. . .ni shiyō
…にしよう。

Japanese food ★★★
washoku
和食

Beef rice bowl ★★★
gyūdon
牛丼
牛丼 (*gyūdon*: beef rice bowl) is a typical Japanese fast food. It is cheap, filling, and very tasty. Famous chain restaurants

include すき家 (*Sukiya*), 吉野家 (*Yoshinoya*), and 松屋 (*Matsuya*).

Egg noodles ★★★
rāmen
ラーメン
I have eaten *rāmen* abroad several times, but they were all very different from real Japanese *rāmen*. Real *rāmen* is elegant and delicate in flavor, and the noodles and broth work together to create a single work of art.

Korean barbecue ★★★
yaki niku
焼き肉
This has little to do with the soul food you are probably accustomed to. Thin slabs of top-grade beef, often marinated, are grilled at your table.

Japanese pancake ★★★
okonomiyaki
お好み焼き
Consisting of a batter with shredded cabbage, *okonomiyaki* is a kind of savory pancake that allows you to add pretty much whatever you feel like: bacon, seafood, veggies, cheese, noodles, kimchi.

Chicken kabobs ★★★
yakitori
焼き鳥
Yakitori is usually sold by street vendors, and comes in a wide variety of forms: chicken breast, chicken wings, chicken cartilage, chicken liver, chicken skin.

Breaded pork ★★★
tonkatsu
とんかつ
Basically, this is a deep-fried pork cutlet.

Japanese stew ★★★

oden

おでん

You know it's winter in Japan when the convenience stores pull out these big vats of broth and start stewing stuff: eggs, potatoes, daikon, tofu, *kamaboko*. Trust me on this: The stuff at 7-Eleven is actually really good.

Soups ★★★

nabemono

鍋物

Nabemono is an umbrella term for a number of soup dishes, including sukiyaki and shabu-shabu.

Tempura ★★★

tenpura

天ぷら

This is like the assorted deep-fry platter.

Chinese food ★★★

chūka ryouri

中華料理

Curry ★★★

karē

カレー

French food ★★★
furansu ryōri
フランス料理
A lot of Japanese cooks actually go to France to study foreign cooking, so French food in Japan can be pretty authentic!

Italian food ★★★
itaria ryōri
イタリア料理
Recently, authentic Italian cuisine has been appearing in Tokyo and elsewhere. So, if you miss Italian food, you can find something satisfying in Japan.

••••••Fast food
fasuto fūdo
ファストフード

Today's busy businessman and fast food are inseparable. Of course, there are many famous fast-food restaurants in Japan.

Let's go to... ★★★
... ikō ze
…行こうぜ。

McDonald's ★★★
makku
マック
The Golden Arches. We have different menu items not available in America, plus all of the classics. We call the マック (*makku*: McDonald's) in Eastern Japan and マクド (*makudo*: McDonald's) in Western Japan.

Mos Burger ★★★
mosu
モス
Mosu is like the Shake Shack of Japanese fast food. They use quality beef and have all sorts of experimental burgers.

Wendy's First Kitchen ★★
fakkin
ファッキン
Though there are not many Wendy's in Japan, they are well known to most Japanese.

Freshness Burger ★★
furesshunesu bāgā
フレッシュネスバーガー
Freshness Burger is kind of a health-conscious burger joint.

Kentucky Fried Chicken ★★
kenta / kentakkī
ケンタ (in Eastern Japan) / ケンタッキー (in Western Japan)
Kentakkī literally means "Kentucky" but is shortened to *kenta* in Eastern Japan.

CHRISTMAS FRIED CHICKEN

Personally, I think Christmas in Japan is a little strange and interesting. This is because in Japan, "Last Christmas," by the English pop duo Wham!, is played all the time in town during Christmas, and some Japanese believe it is an American tradition to spend time at home eating KFC chicken and Christmas cake with their significant other.

•••••Family restaurants
famiresu
ファミレス

Family restaurants in Japan have a drink bar on the menu that offers a variety of soft drinks at low prices. One of the most surprising is that for an additional charge, you can add all-you-can-drink beers, wines, and other alcoholic beverages. Japanese *izakaya* (Japanese-style pubs) also have this all-you-can-drink system, but this may be a business that can only be done in Japan.

Let's go to... ★★★
... ikō ze
…行こうぜ。

Royal Host ★
roiho (roiyaru hosuto)
ロイホ(ロイヤルホスト)
Royal Host is the standard-bearer for all family restaurants. It has a lot of meat-based dishes on the menu.

Denny's ★★
denīzu
デニーズ
As a long-established family restaurant that has been in business for over 50 years, this chain is popular for its hamburgers and other Western-style menu items.

Gusto ★★
gasuto
ガスト
Cheap and easy, Gusto is popular with some college and high school kids.

Saizeriya ★★
saize (saizeriya)
サイゼ(サイゼリヤ)
Saizeriya is a Japanese-Italian fusion family restaurant.

Don ★
suteiki no don → sutedon
ステーキのドン → ステドン
"Don," as this steak house is affectionately called, makes a damn good steak.

Bikkuri Donkey ★
bikkuri donkii → bikudon
びっくりドンキー → びくドン
Bikkuri Donkey specializes in Salisbury steaks, and they do a good job with them.

·····Cafés

kissaten

喫茶店

If you like Starbucks, you must visit Starbucks in Nakameguro (Reserve® Roastery). It occupies a four-story building with a very stylish interior. The terrace overlooks the river and turns into a romantic place at night.

Starbucks ★★★

sutaba

スタバ

Both Japan and US have tall and grande sizes, and they're both about the same. Japan also has an option called "short," which is one size smaller than "tall."

Doutor ★★★

dotōru

ドトール

When I researched the reasons for Doutor's popularity in Japan, many people explained that the locations are good, the prices are low, and the coffee is delicious.

Komeda Coffee ★★★

komeda kōhī

コメダ珈琲

This fashionable cafe has a nationwide presence. The interior is designed to provide a relaxing and comfortable atmosphere.

Tully's ★★★

tarīzu

タリーズ

Tully's is popular because of its selection of high-quality beans and its adherence to the "three principles of freshly roasted, freshly ground, and freshly brewed." I often go to my local Tully's and read books.

CHAPTER 4

FLIRTING JAPANESE

NANPA NIHONGO

ナンパ日本語

I think there are a lot of pickup artists in Japan, especially in city centers. There are places called "pickup spots" where you can find lots of people wanting to pick up others and people who want to be picked up. Unfortunately, I have never actually tried picking someone up so far, but I have friends who are professional pickup artists, so I created this section by listening to their stories and doing some research.

I don't know about other countries, but in Japan, the usual process for a pickup seems to be: approach on the street -> exchange social media -> café -> karaoke[1] -> love hotel.

When mobile phone numbers were in common use, getting a phone number was called "番ゲ (*bangae*)" because it meant getting 電話番号 (*denwa bangou*: a phone number). However, now that many people use LINE (a messaging app like WhatsApp) or Instagram, the term *bangae* is becoming obsolete.

---

1 Getting to know each other at a cafe and going to karaoke to increase physical contact.

••••• Flirting phrases

nanpa furēzu

ナンパフレーズ

Once you've found someone you like, it's time to think about your pickup line. Here, I'll introduce some of the pickup lines most commonly used in Japan. However, the fact that they are commonly used means that just about everyone knows them. So, when you actually go to pick someone up, you'll need to use your own original words. Unless you are super good-looking, you won't succeed in picking someone up if you use worn-out phrases. However, you can learn commonly used expressions and use them to come up with your own lines. So let's start by learning these!

Ask questions

Hello. I heard there's a good cafe nearby. Do you know it?
konnichiwa. kono chikaku ni oishii kafe ga aru tte kiitan desu kedo, shite masu ka
こんにちは。この近くに美味しいカフェがあるって聞いたんですけど、知ってますか?

Excuse me, I heard there's an interesting bookstore nearby. Do you know it?
sumimasen, kono chikaku ni omoshiroi honya ga arutte kiitan desu kedo, gozonjidesuka
すみません、この近くに面白い本屋があるって聞いたんですけど、ご存知ですか?

Add some humor

Excuse me for suddenly talking to you. I didn't expect to meet my future wife.
ano, kyuni hanashikakete sumimasen.masaka jibun no mirai no okusan ni autowa omowa nakute
あの、急に話しかけてすみません。まさか自分の未来の奥さんに会うとは思わなくて。

You dropped something! . . . . . It's my heart.
otoshimono shimashita yo ! . . . . . boku no kokoro desu
落とし物しましたよ!.....僕の心です。

Convey your feelings directly

Hello, I thought you look nice, so I decided to say hi. Would you like to chat a bit?
konnichiwa. suteki da na to omote hanashikakechaimashita. sukoshi ohanashishimasen ka
こんにちは、素敵だなと思って話しかけちゃいました。少しお話ししませんか?

Excuse me, I saw you and I was really curious. Can I talk to you for a bit?
sumimasen, mikakete sugoku ki ni natte. sukoshi ohanashishite mo ii desu ka
すみません、見かけてすごく気になって。少しお話ししてもいいですか?

When picking up women, don't be a creep. For example, if you get rejected or ignored, say "ありがとうございます (*arigatou gozaimasu*: thank you)" to the person in a pleasant way. When talking to someone, you need to be extremely careful not to scare them. Some people say "ブス!(*busu!*: you're ugly!)" the moment they are rejected, but people who say things like that are not gentlemen.

⋯⋯Exchange of contact information
renraku saki koukan
連絡先交換

Going beyond pickup lines, we don't exchange phone numbers or email addresses anymore. There are differences in the apps used for communication in each country.

I've found that the most commonly used apps in Japan are currently LINE and Instagram. Instagram in particular allows you to get to know the other person well, and it's easy to exchange information casually. I personally think it's a little more difficult to exchange information using LINE, as it is mainly a messaging app like WhatsApp.

Let's trade Instagram accounts! ★★★
insta *koukan shiyo*
インスタ交換し!
Instagram translates to インスタグラム but like in the US, a shortened version is commonly used.

I don't want to exchange LINE with you. ★★★
omae to ***rain*** *koukan shitakunai*
お前とライン交換したくない。

WhatsApp isn't really used in Japan. ★
whatsapp wa nihon de amari tsukawareteinai yo
WhatsApp は日本であまり使われていないよ。

Are you still using a phone number and email address? That's so old-fashioned! ★
mada ***denwa bangou*** *to* ***mēru*** *tsukateiru no? jidaiokure da yo*
まだ電話番号とメール使っているの?時代遅れだよ!

••••••Preferences
konomi
好み

People's tastes and preferences are really interesting. There are various things that affect our tastes, such as our environment, genes, experiences, traumas, etc. This chapter talks about picking up girls, so let's introduce some Japanese related to, let's call them "adult tastes." Also, from now on, the content will gradually become more adult. Let's slowly enter the darkness.

Enormous tits ★★★

bakunyuu

爆乳

Bakunyuu (literally "explosive breasts") is a word that refers to large breasts, usually indicating that a woman has extremely large tits. They are the size of anime characters, so they are not actually very common—they are mainly seen in comics, anime, and adult content.

> **I want to go out with a girl with enormous tits at least once in my life!**
> *jinsei de ichido wa* ***bakunyuu*** *no hito to tsukiatte mitai*
> 人生で一度は爆乳の人と付き合ってみたい！

Big tits ★★★

kyonyuu

巨乳

Kyonyuu is a slang term referring to a woman with relatively large breasts. It is a more common term that does not give the same extreme impression.

> **Big tits save the world.**
> ***kyonyuu*** *wa sekai o sukuu*
> 巨乳は世界を救う。

Beautiful tits ★★★

binyuu

美乳

Binyuu is a compliment that refers to beautiful breasts. They are judged comprehensively based on factors such as shape and areola. However, the criteria differ from person to person.

> **A person with beautiful tits has a beautiful heart, too.**
> ***binyuu*** *no hito wa kokoro mo utsukushii*
> 美乳の人は心も美しい。

Small tits (flat-chested) ★★★

hinnyuu

貧乳

Literally, "poor tits." *Hinnyuu* is slang for a woman with small breasts. Some women are concerned about having small breasts, so be careful how you use this term. It is sometimes referred to as まな板 (*manaita*: a cutting board) or 絶壁 (*zeppeki*: a sheer cliff).

> **People's tastes change with age, but eventually everyone ends up liking small tits.**
> *hito no konomi wa nenrei ni yotte kawaru ga, yagate mina* ***hinnyu*** *zuki ni ikitsuku*
> 人の好みは年齢によって変わるが、やがて皆貧乳好きに行き着く。

Mature woman/MILF ★★★
jukujo
熟女
Jukujo is a term used to refer to an older woman, often used to describe an attractive, mature woman, but with sexual connotations.

> **The appeal of MILFs cannot be summed up in a few words.**
> ***jukujo*** *no yosa wa hitokoto de wa katarenai*
> 熟女の良さは一言では語れない

Women who are around 30 years old ★★
arasā
アラサー
Arasā is slang for a woman in her early 30s, derived from "around 30." Generally, it refers to a woman who is socially independent and values her career and personal life.

> **My younger sister is so worried about turning around 30, she can't sleep at night.**
> *boku no imouto to wa* ***arasā*** *ni naru no ga shimpai de yoru mo nemu re nai*
> 僕の妹とはアラサーになるのが心配で夜も眠れない。

Virgin (female) ★★★
shojo
処女
Shojo refers to a woman who has not had sexual experience. Depending on the context, it may also emphasize purity or innocence.

There's a big difference between "liking virgins" and "liking little girls."
shojo *ga suki to* ***shoujo*** *ga suki wa zenzen chigau imi da yo*
処女が好きと**少女**が好きは全然違う意味だよ。

Virgin (male) ★★★
dōtei
童貞
Dōtei refers to a man who has not had sexual experience.

Is it true that there are women who like virgins?
dōtei *zuki na josei ga sonzai suru to iu no wa, honto desu ka*
童貞好きな女性が存在するというのは、本当ですか?

••••• Social types
iroiro na hito
いろいろな人

< BURIKKO ★★★
ぶりっ子
A ditz. Literally, *burikko* means "a girl who pretends." Like her American counterpart, a *burikko* isn't actually ditzy. A *burikko* knows her cute points and tries to use them to her advantage to control men. And the most frightening thing is that, even though men know this, they are captivated by the overly cute gestures of the woman who is playing the role of a klutz, and as a result, they end up falling in love with her and becoming her obedient slave.

< GYARU ★★★
ギャル
This is a typical social type in Japan—girls with tanned skin, blonde hair, flashy clothes in fluorescent colors, and white makeup around their eyes. There are various levels of *gyaru*, and the most extreme type is called "*yamanba*" (now almost extinct). Unfortunately, these types of *gyaru* are not very common nowadays. The *gyaru* of today have a little less make-up and are

more modern but still have tanned skin. They are mainly found in Shibuya, so if you walk around Shibuya, you're sure to spot some.

< YANKEE ★★★
ヤンキー

Yankee refers to a gangster-type boy. Like *gyarus*, they have blonde hair, tanned skin, and statistically tend to have low levels of education. If you want to know more about *yankees*, you should watch the anime series *Tokyo Revengers*.[2]

< OTAKU ★★★
オタク

The word *otaku* appears often in English. If you're familiar with the word, you might think of it as meaning "someone who's super obsessed with Japanese anime or manga." But actually in Japan the word just means "a nerd who is super obsessed with their hobby." The hobby could be anything, it doesn't need to be Japan related. The typical image is of someone who stays up all night, playing games or watching anime with the lights off in their apartment. In fact, I also made a YouTube video of myself dressed up as an *otaku*, so if you Google "Onomappu Otaku,"

---

2 By the way, I made a YouTube video of my experience meeting a *yankee* while cosplaying as a Yankee. Search for "Onomappu Yankee" or visit https://youtu.be/ks-fFvyNFYQ.

you will better understand its meaning. The word *otakuto* used to have a slightly critical meaning, but now I think that meaning is almost gone. Many people say that if they are passionate about something, they are an *otaku* themselves. For example, people who like trains are called "train *otaku*," and people who like celebrities are called "idol *otaku*" (in Japan, celebrities are referred to as "idols"). In my opinion, these people deserve our awe and respect. They don't care what society says, and they are completely immersed in their interests.

< ŌERU OL ★★

OL

Ōeru ("*OL*") stands for "office lady." Typically, there are many jobs that involve administrative tasks such as document creation, data entry, telephone response, and schedule management. It has a positive image as a job for a professional woman who works hard, but on the other hand, it is sometimes seen as a job that women do until they get married, and career-oriented women may feel uncomfortable with it.

< BABAA ★★

ババア

Babaa is a term used to refer to an old lady in a rude way. The more polite way to say it is *obasan*, but women don't like being called old, so it's best not to say it anyway. On the other hand, the word *ojisan* (old man) doesn't have as bad a meaning as *obasan*. Women tend to have higher mental ages, so some women who are bored with their age group like *ojisan* (old man).

< HIKIKOMORI ★★

引きこもり

The abbreviation for *hikikomori* is *hikkī*, which means "shut-in." In most cases, there is some kind of traumatic event that causes them to shut themselves away at home and even dislike being exposed to sunlight. However, now it is also used in cases where the meaning is lighter than the original meaning. For example, it is used when someone says that they will become *hikikomori* and watch Netflix over the weekend.

·····Pickup terms

nanpa yougo

ナンパ用語

There are certain words that are used by people who pick up a lot of women. Here, words that even ordinary people have heard before are marked with ★★★, and words that only pickup artists would understand are marked with ★. In other words, if you use a ★ word and the other person understands it, then that person is likely to be either a pickup artist or someone interested in pickup artists.

One-night stand ★★★
wan naito
ワンナイト

It would be great to have a one-night stand with that girl.
*ano ko to **wan naito** dekitara saiko da na*
あの子と**ワンナイト**できたら最高だな。

Being annoying ★
gudaru
グダる

I tried talking with her but she seemed annoyed so I gave up.
*Kanojo to hanasou to shitakedo, kanojo ga **gudatta** node akirameta*
彼女と話そうとしたけど、彼女が**グダった**ので諦めた。

Taking out ★★
tsuredashi
連れ出し

I took her out of the club, but I couldn't get her to the hotel.
kurabu kara ***tsuredashita*** *no ni, hoteru made ikenakatta*
クラブから**連れ出した**のに、ホテルまで行けなかった

Having sex on the same day as meeting ★
sokuru
即る
即 means immediately.

Yesterday I got to know two people and ended up having sex with them.
kinou wa futari ***sokutta*** *yo*
昨日は2人**即った**よ

Having sex on the second meeting ★
junsoku
準即

That girl was very guarded, but I was able to have sex with her the next time we met.
ano ko wa gado ga katakatta kedo, ***junsoku*** *deki ta yo*
あの子はガードが固かったけど、**準即**できたよ。

Reverse pickup
gyaku nan
逆ナン
The term "reverse pickup" refers to the act of a woman picking up a man, as opposed to the usual situation where a man picks up a woman. In other words, it is the opposite of the usual pattern of picking up. When a woman actively approaches a man, it can show both a break from traditional romantic patterns and equality of power. In recent anime trends, there are stories where strong girls protect weak boys. But it can also be said that reverse pickup is a way for women to express their feelings to men. I'm waiting for a reverse pickup, so please contact me anytime. (Just kidding . . . maybe.)

•••••Types of pick-up lines
nanpa no syurui
ナンパの種類

A phrase you often hear is "ストナン (*suto nan*: street pickups)." This culture still exists. *Suto nan* is when you approach women on the street. There are also ネトナン (*neto nan*: online pickups) on sites like X and Instagram. Some people have success with クラナン (*kura nan*: night club pickups). Each club has a different purpose. Establishments where pickups often take place are called ナンパ箱 (*nanpa bako*: a pickup box), but according to someone I know, it's difficult to talk to people in pickup boxes because they are always so crowded.

Street pickup ★★★
suto nan
ストナン

Online pickup ★★★
neto nan
ネトナン

Night club pickup ★★
kura nan
クラナン

•••••Flattery
oseji
お世辞

In Japan, flattery is using words that differ from one's actual thoughts and opinions in order to improve the other person's feelings or evaluation of you. In particular, it refers to the use of words of praise or goodwill in order to please the other person. This behavior is often employed in social or formal situations in order to protect the other person's self-esteem or to smooth over relationships. It's sometimes said Japan has a culture of flattery. As a Japanese person, I also think this is the case. However, if flattery is used excessively, it can give the impression of insincerity. Let me give you a few examples of everyday uses of flattery in Japan.

Mr. President! Your hair looks great today too!
shachou ! kyou mo sono kamigata niatte imasu ne
社長！今日もその髪型似合っていますね！

You're so cool. I've never seen anyone so cool before.
totemo kakkoii desu ne. konna kakkoii hito, imamade mita koto nai desu
とてもかっこいいですね。こんなかっこいい人、今まで見たことないです。

You're definitely popular, aren't you? What's your secret?
anata tte zettai moteru yo ne. hiketsu wa nani
あなたって絶対モテるよね？秘訣は何？

•••••Confession culture
kokuhaku bunka
告白文化

Do you know about Japan's culture of confession? A confession is when a man or woman tells a person they like how they feel about them. In anime, it's common for a girl to give her crush a letter, telling him to meet her after school. Of course, there are also cases where the roles of boy and girl are reversed. I have also experienced being confessed to, and have told this story on my YouTube channel.[3]

---

3 Check it out here: https://youtu.be/kE-wapusqLc.

·····Words used when dating

dēto no kotoba

デートの言葉

I have a very memorable story from when I was in junior high school. One day, a boy who I was good friends with in the same class, received a letter from a girl he liked, and he was so happy he almost cried. The letter said he should go to the back of the gym after school. However, when he actually went to the place, it wasn't the girl he liked, but another girl who was completely not his type. The girl he liked had only helped hand over the letter for her friend.

A date ★★★
dēto
デート

I'd like to go on a date with that girl.
*ano ko to **dēto** ni ikitai na*
あの子とデートに行きたいな。

Go out with. . . ★★★
. . .to tsukiau
. . .と付き合う

I want to go out with the most beautiful woman in the world.
*konoyo de ichiban no bijo **to tsukiaitai***
この世で一番の美女と付き合いたい。

Break up ★★★
wakareru
別れる

I never thought we'd break up after being together for three years.
*3 nen mo tsukiatta noni masaka **wakareru** nante omowanakatta*
3年も付き合ったのにまさか**別れる**なんて思わなかった。

Being rejected ★★★
furareta
振られた

I told her I liked her, but she rejected me.
boku wa kanojo ni suki to tsutaeta ga furareta
僕は彼女に好きと伝えたが振られた。

Confess ★★★
kokuhaku suru
告白する

The best way to convey your feelings to someone is to make a confession.
aite ni jibun no omoi o tsutaeru ni wa kokuhaku ichiban da
相手に自分の思いを伝えるには告白一番だ。

Cheat ★★★
uwaki suru
浮気する

If you cheat on your wife, you'll be executed.
uwaki o shitara shikei da
浮気をしたら死刑だ。
This is similar to the English phrase, "My wife is gonna kill me."

•••••Where Japanese people hang out
nihonjin no asobiba
日本人の遊び場

Japanese people like to drink. The culture of drinking together (飲み会: *nomikai*) is very distinctive; after work at the office, people often go to a pub with their boss or colleagues, to talk about things they couldn't while busy at work.

Also, there is a certain number of Japanese people who, for genetic reasons, cannot take alcohol well, and I am one of them. After just a few sips of beer, my face turns bright red. And I get drunk quickly. Being a lightweight has its benefits!

When you go out in Japan, you should know that Japan is relatively safe; for example, women can walk alone at night in most neighborhoods. Of course, there are dangerous places everywhere, so please don't go near places that look dangerous.

< IZAKAYA ★★★
居酒屋

The standard Japanese drinking establishment that's basically a cross between a bar and a restaurant. Most of your drinking will be done in one of these.

That izakaya has disgusting food, but the drinks are cheap.
asoko no ***izakaya*** *wa meshi ga mazui kedo sake ga yasui*
あそこの居酒屋は飯がまずいけど酒が安い。

< KARAOKE ★★★
カラオケ

Small, private karaoke rooms are rented by the hour.

Yesterday we sang every Beatles song in the karaoke joint.
kinō wa ***karaoke*** *de bītoruzu no zenkyoku utatte shimatta*
昨日はカラオケでビートルズの全曲歌ってしまった。

We Japanese don't dance very often, but we often go to karaoke with friends. There, by singing songs together and getting into the rhythm, we deepen our connections with one another.

< KURABU ★★★
クラブ

Loud music and drinks. Often categorized by the type of music being DJ'ed: hip-hop club, reggae club, punk club.

Do you know a good club for picking up rich, handsome men?
kanemochi no ikemen o getto dekisō na ***kurabu*** *shitteru*
金持ちのイケメンをゲットできそうな**クラブ**知ってる?

< GĒSEN ★★★
ゲーセン

A video game arcade. Swallow your pride, man—nothing beats a good game of drunken *Tekken*.

Last night I got so drunk I wound up spending a lot of money at the arcade.
kinō wa nomisugite ***gēsen*** *de takusan okane tsukacchatta*
昨日は飲みすぎてゲーセンでたくさんお金つかっちゃった。

< FAMIRESU ★★★
ファミレス

Short for "family restaurant," this implies Denny's or some other chain restaurant. They have good food and serve alcohol! Often open 24 hours, for when a night gets really sloppy. You can find a list of these in Chapter 3.

Let's wait for the first train at a family restaurant.
famiresu *de asaichi no densha o matō*
ファミレスで朝一の電車を待とう。

< MANGA KISSA ★★★
漫画喫茶

A 24-hour internet café/comic book library. You can pay by the hour to read, watch movies, send drunken mass emails, or just sleep until the morning train. Not a party place, per se, but a good place to kill time between parties. Free soft drinks.

There's nothing to do till the club opens up—wanna hit up a manga kissa?
kurabu ga aku made yarukoto nai kara ***manga kissa*** *demo ittemiru*
クラブが開くまでやることないから漫画喫茶でもいってみる?

< BĀ, NOMIYA ★★★

バー・飲み屋

A Western-style bar.

< SUNAKKU ★

スナック

A bar with flirty waitresses. Middle-aged dudes love these places. Although the number of stores has declined in recent years, it is still a place where middle-aged and older people can relax.

< KYABAKURA ★★★

キャバクラ

A place where you can drink with young, beautiful women. Most places charge by time slots of 40 to 60 minutes. If you see a good-looking girl, you can treat her to expensive drinks.

< HOSUTESU KURABU ★★★

ホストクラブ

Ladies, this one's for you! This is the male version of kyabakura. Many good-looking men will praise you. It may seem like paradise, but before you know it, you'll run out of money.

< SUTORIPPU ★

ストリップ

A strip club.

< NOMIKAI ★★★

飲み会

A drinking party. Usually takes place at an *izakaya*.

< ENKAI ★★

宴会

Same as *nomikai*, but usually celebrating a specific thing.

< HANAMI ★★
花見

Sakura flower viewing. People enjoy spreading out blankets or tarps under the cherry blossom trees, eating delicious food and drinking delicious drinks. It is a great moment to enjoy talking together amidst the dancing petals of the cherry blossoms.

< DONKI ★★★
ドンキ

Welcome to Don Quixote, the Japanese Wal-Mart. Not a place where you want to go party, but it's open 24 hours, and you can always find interesting folks wandering the aisles at 3 a.m.

< NIJIKAI ★★★
二次会

The after party. This can be held at any of the above establishments and often involves missing your train, puking on your friend's shoes, and hitting on nameless coworkers.

< GŌKON/KOMPA ★★★
合コン / コンパ

A dude invites his male friends, and a girl invites her female friends, and everybody gets drunk together. At some point the girls go to the bathroom and decide who gets who. Basically, it's an organized version of Friday night at the bar.

< ŌRU ★★★
オール

This means to "stay up all night." But in many cases, it means "Fuck the last train, we're drinking till morning," which happens more often than not.

< YAMANOTE SEN GĒMU ★
山手線ゲーム

A drinking game where you go around in a circle and say the names of stations on the Yamanote Line. When somebody fucks up, they drink. There are a million other possible themes, like the names of prefectures or of foreign actresses. It's so old-fashioned now.

< ŌSAMA GĒMU ★★
王様ゲーム
This is basically the Japanese equivalent of "Truth or Dare." Kind of childish and dumb, unless you're drunk enough, then it's right on your level.

••••• Booze

saké

酒

Cheers to. . . ! ★★★
. . .ni kanpai
. . .に乾杯!

How about a drink? ★★
ippai ikaga
一杯いかが?

. . .brew! ★★
mugishu. . .
麦酒. . .

You got beer on tap? ★★★
***nama bīru** arimasuka*
生ビールありますか?
"Beer on tap" in Japan implies a light pilsner.

(Can I have) a pint of beer, please?
namachū kudasai
生中ください?
"Namachū" is the standard beer order—a medium-sized (pint) glass from the tap.

Know somewhere we can drink a microbrew? ★
*dokka **jibīru** nomeru mise wakaru*
どっか地ビール飲める店わかる?

Hot saké gets me really drunk, man. ★★
atsukan *wa mechakucha yō kara na*
熱燗はめちゃくちゃ酔うからな。
Atsukan is heated saké, usually drunk in the winter, and usually cheaper than the drier saké you drink cold.

Why don't you chug that saké? ★
sono nihonshu o ***ikkinomi*** *shitara?*
その日本酒を一気飲みしたら?
Now, in Japan chugging alcohol is widely considered something one should never do. In fact, several people have died as a result, and the boss who made them do it was fired from their company.

Chug! Chug! Chug! ★
ikki ikki ikki!
一気一気一気!

Let's drink until the last train. ★★
shūden *made nomō ze*
終電まで飲もうぜ。

I'll drink until I vomit. ★★
haku *suru made nomu zo*
吐くまで飲むぞ。

If you're going to barf, do it in the toilet. ★★
gero *surunara toire de yare*
ゲロするならトイレでやれ。

Other drinks that Japanese people enjoy:

Shōchū (potato liquor—drunk by the pros)
焼酎

Chūhai (a cocktail with *shōchū*)
酎ハイ

Until a generation ago, there were drinking games and drinking songs, but now it seems that you almost never see or hear them. In fact, I've never seen them either. Because chugging and drunk driving are strictly restricted in society, naturally, people don't get as crazy about drinking as they used to, and now those kinds of customs have disappeared.

••••••Wasted

deisui

泥酔

Whatever, man—you aren't going to remember any of these vocabulary words when you're sprawled out on the tatami mats, breathing fire. But maybe this will inspire some nice hangover thoughts as you sit there trying to remember what happened last night.

I'm starting to get. . .
. . .shite kichatta
. . .してきちゃった。

. . .buzzed. ★★★
horoyoi. . .
ほろ酔い . . .

. . .a little tipsy—oh no! ★★★
yabai chotto fura fura. . .
ヤバい、ちょっとフラフラ . . .

. . .a bit drunk. ★★★
yopparatta kanji ga. . .
酔っぱらった感じが . . .

. . . smashed.
★★★
beron beron. . .
べろんべろん . . .

CHAPTER 5

COUPLE JAPANESE

KAPPURU DE NO NIHONGO

カップル日本語

There is a stereotype that Japanese people will confess their feelings after the third date. In reality, it doesn't have to be the third date, but if a woman has been on a number of dates with a man and the subject of becoming a couple has not come up, she may become anxious and wonder if he is serious or just playing around. This may seem strange to people from overseas. But for Japanese people, the hurdle to dating together is low whereas the hurdle to having sex is high. Although things are getting more modern, this is still a deeply rooted part of Japanese culture.

For this reason, we get to know each other a little first, and if we think it's going well, we actually go and try things out. During this time, if things go well, some people get married, and if not, some people break up.

·····Dating spots
dēto supotto
デートスポット

In this section, I will explain some of the places that Japanese people often go on dates. The Japanese word for date (デート：*dēto*) has two meanings: The first refers to going out before becoming a couple, and the second refers to going out together after becoming a couple. The spots I introduce here are for the first kind of date – since that is the situation you will struggle with the most.

< EIGAKAN ★★★
映画館
This means a "movie theater." A classic first-date spot!

< SUIZOKUKAN ★★★
水族館
This means an "aquarium." You'll never run out of things to talk about here, with all of the interesting sea creatures.

< DĀTSU ★★
ダーツ
This means "darts." Darts are a good option if you want to enjoy something interactive. The game aspect makes it exciting, and you can play while having a relaxed conversation.

< TĒMA KAFE ★★
テーマ カフェ
There are all kinds of specialty cafes in Japan, such as planetarium cafes. For example, planetarium cafes are a little dark inside, and if you look up you can see a planetarium projected onto the ceiling. There are also many other interesting cafes, such as cafes that use projection mapping and camp cafes, so please check them out online.

< DASSHUTSU GĒMU ★★
脱出ゲーム

It's an escape room, which is a game where you solve puzzles using various props to get out of a room within a certain amount of time. It takes a bit of courage to ask someone you've just met to go to an escape game, but I think it's easier to ask on a second date. I think it's also a lot of fun to go with friends.

< IRUMINĀSHON ★★
イルミネーション

If you're going on a date in winter in Japan, I strongly recommend going to see the illuminations where the night scenery is lit up by many small colored lights, creating the shapes of flowers, various famous characters, etc. The illuminations in Japan are absolutely stunning. I recommend you take a look at some pictures online. Personally, I like the illuminations at Ashikaga Flower Park, and I go there almost every year. The winter weather can be very cold, but if you drink a cup of warm cocoa while you're there, you'll feel happy.

< BŌDO GĒMU ★★
ボードゲーム

This means a "board game." This is a good way to see the other person's personality and decide whether or not they are the best partner for you in the future. (Are they a sore loser?)

< SONOTA ★★★
その他

Other than that, Japanese often go to カラオケ (*karaoke*) and 居酒屋 (*izakaya*), like the ones I mentioned earlier. We also often go to マック(マクドナルド:McDonald's) and スタバ(スターバックス:Starbucks).

•••••Comedy
owarai
お笑い

Let's talk a little about Japanese comedy here. Japanese people really like comedy, and it's not uncommon for couples to have conversations with each other in the style of a comic dialogue. This is good to know if you're looking to explore beyond "textbook Japanese."

Essential comedy words

The following is the classic response to a joke. If someone makes a bad pun, or pokes fun at you, just say "*Nande yanen*!" There is no English word for the literal meaning of the word. This expression is originally from the Kansai dialect and it's meaning is "What the fuck! (How can you be so silly?)". Kansai people are famous for being good at telling jokes. In fact many Japanese comedians are Kansai people, and they often say on TV in response to other people's jokes, "*Nande yanen*!" and this became a widely used response to jokes. So, if your friend says to you, "It's going to rain today, but I didn't bring an umbrella!" you can say, "*Nande yanen*! (You know it, why didn't you bring it!)"

What the fuck! ★★★
nande yanen
なんでやねん！

Make fun of ★★
tsukkomi
突っ込み
A *tsukkomi* is a joke at someone's expense. You notice something funny about someone, and make a *tsukkomi* about it.

Stop making fun of me!
sonna ni tsukkomu na
そんなに突っ込むな！

Are you stupid?! ★★
aho ka
アホか?!

Drinking Coke through your nose—are you stupid?!
hana kara kora nomu toka – omae ***aho ka***
鼻からコーラ飲むとか、お前アホか?!

Punch line ★★
ochi
オチ

This story has no punch line!
ochi *ga naijan kono hanashi*
オチがないじゃん、この話!
Don't always expect Japanese jokes to have them!

Joke (a gag) ★★
gyagu
ギャグ
親父ギャグ (*oyaji gyagu*: old man jokes) are famous for being very lame. However, sometimes they are so lame they are actually funny.

Horrendously bad joke ★
oyaji gyagu
親父ギャグ

••••• Couple onomatopoeia
kappuru onomatope
カップルオノマトペ

I think all languages have some onomatopoeia, but Japanese has an incredibly large number of onomatopoetic expressions. Japanese onomatopoeia is cute, easy to use, and very convenient. Furthermore, because words and sensations are deeply connected, we Japanese feel a sense of familiarity with foreigners who can use onomatopoeia. I created Onomappu on YouTube to introduce Japanese onomatopoeia because I wanted to share this wonderful attribute of our language with others. Here, I will introduce some typical Japanese uses of onomatopoeia that often appear in romantic relationships.

Onomatopoeia attempts to express what people feel through the sounds of words. For example, the sound of the heart pumping blood can be translated into Japanese as "ドキドキ (*doki doki*)."

Oh my God, you are so cute, I can't stop my heart from pounding!
dou shiyou, kimi ga kawai sugite ***doki doki*** *ga tomaranai*
どうしよう、君がかわいすぎてドキドキが止まらない!

Swoon ★★★
kyun kyun
キュンキュン
Kyun kyun is a word that expresses the sweet feelings and nervousness that come with being in love or experiencing romance. It expresses the excitement and happiness that you feel when you experience or say something cute. There is also another word, "キュン死にする (*kyun shi ni suru*)," which means to die from the feeling (LOL!).

Why does my heart flutter when I look at you?
naze, anata o miru to ***kyun kyun*** *suru no*
なぜ、あなたを見るとキュンキュンするの?

Thump thump ★★★
doki doki
ドキドキ
Doki doki refers to the feeling of your heart beating fast due to excitement or nervousness. In the context of romance, it refers to the elation and nervousness you feel when you meet the person you like or during special moments. You can see my YouTube video about *doki doki*, too.[4]

---

4 You can see my video about *doki doki* here: https://www.youtube.com/watch?v=qXoqOvJ9pBE.

It makes me nervous, like my heart is racing to dance with the person I like.
suki na hito to isshoni dansu o suru no wa doki doki suru
好きな人と一緒にダンスをするのはドキドキする。

Lovey-dovey ★★★
labu labu
ラブラブ

Labu labu refers to couples or lovers who have a deep and sweet atmosphere of mutual affection. It expresses a state of being in a very good relationship with your partner, one that is overflowing with affection.

They are always so lovey-dovey.
karera wa itsumo ***labu labu*** *da*
彼らはいつもラブラブだ。

PDA (public display of affection) ★★★
icha icha
イチャイチャ

Icha icha refers to the way that lovers or couples exchange sweet words and expressions of affection, or touch each other's skin. It expresses the idea of spending a sweet time in an intimate atmosphere. It has a different nuance from the English term "PDA," but there isn't a direct translation.

Those two seem really close. Are they dating?
ano futari, ***icha icha*** *shite ite nakayoi ne. tsukiatte iru no*
あの二人、イチャイチャしていて仲良いね。付き合っているの?

Naive love ★★
ubu na koi
ウブな恋

Although it is not an onomatopoetic word, the phrase *ubu na koi* (ウブな恋: naive love) also exists. It refers to a pure and innocent romantic relationship. It expresses the state of being inexperienced and in love.

There was a time when I loved someone with pure innocence.
*watashi mo **ubu na koi** o shite ita koro ga atta*
私もウブな恋をしていた頃があった。

••••• Displaying affection
aijou hyougen
愛情表現

Holding hands ★★★
te wo tsunagu
手をつなぐ
In particular, the way of holding each finger between each other's fingers is called 恋人繋ぎ (*koibito tsunagi*: holding hands with fingers interlocked).

Wink ★★
uinku
ウインク

Patting someone on the head ★★
atama wo naderu
頭を撫でる

Hug ★★★
hagu
ハグ

Kissing ★★★
kisu
キス

Smooch ★★★
chuu
ちゅう

I wanna smooch you!
boku wa kimi to chuu shitai
僕は君とちゅうしたい!

A blown kiss ★
nage kissu
投げキッス

French kiss ★★
furenchi kisu
フレンチキス

Deep kiss ★★
dīpu kisu
ディープキス

Tongue kiss ★
bero chuu
ベロちゅう
Bero chuu is a graphic way of saying "deep kiss." You can use it in a sexy situation, but it's too direct and a little over the top in normal ones.

••••• Marriage
kekkon
結婚

These days, there are many ways to interact with a partner, and marriage is not always the goal, as it used to be. However, many people still marry their partners, so let's learn some Japanese related to marriage.

Marriage ★★★
kekkon
結婚

Common law marriage ★★
jijitsu kon
事実婚

Same-sex marriage ★★★
dousei kon
同性婚

Divorced ★★★
rikon
離婚

Remarried ★★★
saikon
再婚

Cohabitation ★★★
dousei
同棲

Living apart ★★★
bekkyo
別居

JAPANESE BLOOD-TYPE PERSONALITY DIVINATION

In Japan there's a belief that blood type affects a person's personality and behavior patterns. This is known as "血液型占い (*ketsueki gata uranai*: blood-type fortune-telling)," and I used to discuss it with my friends a lot in the past. However, please regard this blood-type fortune-telling just as a source of fun, as it has little scientific basis.

Blood type A
ēgata
A型
Characteristics: Serious and responsible
Behavior patterns: They value rules and like to keep things in order. They are very attentive to their surroundings but are stubborn and easily angered.

Blood type B
bīgata
B型
Characteristics: Free-spirited and self-paced
Behavior patterns: They hate being constrained and being suppressed. They have a flexible way of thinking and can accept different ideas. They are full of humanity but are not good at reading other people's minds. By the way, I'm type B.

Blood type O
ōgata
O型
Characteristics: Sociable, positive; has leadership skills
Behavior patterns: Cheerful and active, they think positively even when faced with difficulties. They value relationships and place importance on reliability. However, they give up easily when they think they are going to lose.

Blood type AB
ēbīgata
AB型
Characteristics: Dry and rational
Behavior patterns: They are flexible and think things through logically and according to the situation. They are good at analysis, have a very strong ability to criticize, and are good at being sarcastic. They want a job that allows them to live their hobbies.

CHAPTER 6

BODY JAPANESE

KARADA NI KANSURU NIHONGO

体に関する日本語

Before we start studying the full range of erotic Japanese in Chapter 6, let's study some Japanese related to the human body. As is probably the case in other countries, it is considered especially rude to talk about a person's body shape. Japanese women tend to dislike being asked direct questions about their weight, age, marriage, or children, as well as their body shape. If you ask these kinds of questions at work, you could be accused of sexual harassment and even fired, so be very careful. Japanese men are not quite so strict at the moment, but who knows what the future may bring?

Ecstatic face ★★★
ahe gao
アヘ顔
A facial expression that shows someone is immersed in pleasure, with a dazed look on their face, like they're in a state of euphoria. It appears in adult manga and anime, and is so popular with some people that it has even appeared on printed T-shirts overseas.

Feminine face ★
mesu gao
メス顔
The face of a woman when she is sexually aroused. The word "メス (*mesu*: female)" is used for animals, giving it a more animalistic connotation. It is used when a person's face is flushed.

Orgasm face ★★
iki gao
イキ顔
The face of a person while they're having an orgasm. It is used when a person's eyes and mouth are half-open due to extreme pleasure.

•••••The Japanese ideal
nihonjin no risō
日本人の理想

It may be strange to talk about ideals for the human body in the modern world. This is because, in a world where diversity is valued and individuality is respected, everyone has a different idea of what an ideal body is. Therefore, here we will explain words that are relatively often used as compliments in Japan. Of course, depending on the person and the timing, they may not always be compliments, so be careful.

He/She has . . .
kare/kanojo wa . . .
彼・彼女は. . .

. . . a small face ★★★
. . . kao ga chīsai
. . .顔が小さい

. . . big eyes ★★★
. . . ookina me wo shiteiru
. . .大きな目をしている

. . . round eyes ★★
. . . kurikuri na me wo shiteiru
. . .くりくりな目をしている

. . . big nose ★★★
. . . hana ga takai
. . .鼻が高い

. . . a good figure ★★★
. . . sutairu ga ī
. . .スタイルがいい

He/She is . . .
kare/kanojo wa . . .
彼・彼女は. . .

. . . cute (guys and girls, but mostly girls) ★★★
. . . kawaī
. . .かわいい

. . . pretty ★★★
. . . kirei
. . .きれい

. . . beautiful ★★★
. . . utsukushī
. . .美しい

. . . cool ★★★
. . . kakko ī
. . .カッコイイ

. . . slim ★★
. . . surimu
. . .スリム

. . . skinny (mostly girls) ★★
. . . hosoi
. . .細い

. . . solidly built (guys) ★★
. . . gacchiri shiteiru
. . .がっちりしている

. . . stylish ★★★
. . . oshare
. . .おしゃれ

. . . popular ★★★
. . . mote mote
. . .モテモテ

. . . hip ★
. . . iketeru
. . .イケてる

JAPANESE VALUES

NIHONJIN NO KATIKA

日本人の価値観

There is always a topic among Japanese women about what kind of man is ideal. Of course, it goes without saying that everyone's idea of the ideal is different, but there are certain standards that many women want men to have. Here, we will introduce them.

"3K" from a while ago (during the "economic bubble era" in Japan; around 1990)

Japanese people like to abbreviate everything. Here, we will introduce the ideal man, known as 3K, using the initial letters of each Japanese word that described him during the bubble era: ***kougakureki, koushuunyuu,*** and ***koushintyou.*** Btw the bubble era was a time when real estate and stock prices rose rapidly due to overheated investment and consumption, and the rate of growth was much faster than actual economic growth.

Highly educated
Kougakureki
高学歴

High income
Koushuunyuu
高収入

Tall height
Koushintyou
高身長

"New 3K" of the current era

Unlike in the past, now compatibility and stability with a partner are more important than money or appearance. Many Japanese have realized that just because someone has a high level of education doesn't mean they will be rich, and furthermore, just because someone is rich doesn't mean they will be happy. They also believe it is more important to have the same financial sense with a partner. Also, even if you are currently earning a high income, it will be difficult to continue living together if the couple's income is not stable, so it is desirable to have stable employment. The most important thing is that your values match. As time progresses, everyone's spiritual level tends to rise, and they become aware of the greatness of compassion and love. I think you can see a glimpse of such a change here.

Same moral values
Kachikan ga issho
価値観が一緒

Same sense of financial values
Kinsen kankaku ga issho
金銭感覚が一緒

Stable employment
Koyou keitai ga antei
雇用形態が安定

•••••The Japanese ugly
nijon no busaiku
日本の「ぶさいく」

He/She has a . . .
kare/kanojo wa . . .
彼・彼女は. . .

. . . round face ★★
. . . kao ga marui
. . .顔が丸い

. . . pig nose ★★
. . . butappana da
. . .ぶたっぱなだ

. . . short legs ★★★
. . . ashi ga mijikai
. . .足が短い

. . . bad figure ★★
. . . sutairu ga warui
. . .スタイルが悪い

He/She is . . .
kare/kanojo wa . . ..
彼・彼女は. . .

. . . ugly ★★
. . . busaiku
. . .ぶさいく

. . . ugly (more casual) ★★★
. . . busu
. . .ぶす

. . . lame ★★★
. . . dasai
. . .ださい

. . . unpopular ★★★
. . . motenai
. . .モテない

. . . unhip ★
. . . iketenai
. . .イケてない

. . . husky ★
. . . kobutori
. . .小太り

. . . chubby ★★★
. . . pocchari
. . .ぽっちゃり

. . . fat ★★★
. . . debu
. . .でぶ

. . . chunky ★★
. . . debuccho
. . .でぶっちょ

. . . messy ★★★
. . . kitanai
. . .汚い

Other body types

He/She is . . .
kare/kanojo wa . . .
彼・彼女は. . .

. . . little (not just height—altogether small) ★★★
. . . kogara
. . .小柄

. . . ripped ★★★
. . . gottsui
. . .ごっつい

. . . delicate ★★★
. . . kyasha
. . .華奢

. . . tanned ★★★
. . . hiyake shiteiru
. . .日焼けしている

. . . pale ★★
. . . aoshiroi
. . .青白い

. . . scrawny ★★
. . . gari gari shiteiru
. . .ガリガリしている

. . . hunched over (bad posture) ★★
. . . nekoze
. . .猫背

Looks like you're getting a bit of a beer belly there. ★★★
*chotto **bīruppara** ni natta ne*
ちょっと**ビールっぱら**になったね。

I gotta go on a diet. ★★★
daietto shinakya
ダイエットしなきゃ。

Check out my sixpack! ★★★
*hora **fukkin** wareteru daro*
ほら、**腹筋**割れてるだろ！

Man, you are totally ripped! ★★★
*omae kin'niku **mori mori** jan*
お前、筋肉**モリモリ**じゃん！

·····Genitalia, etc.
seiki nado
性器など

Dick ★★★
chinko
ちんこ

Dick (in a cute way) ★
(o)chinpo
（お）ちんぽ
With お, it's more polite to the dick.

Peepee (children often use) ★★
chin chin
ちんちん

My thing (penis indirectly) ★★★
asoko
あそこ
We often say "THERE: あそこ" when we don't want to say it too clearly. If you like men, you can ask them politely like this:

> **Hey, can I touch your thing?**
> *nee, kimi no* ***asoko*** *sawattemo ii*
> ねえ、君のあそこ触ってもいい?

Penis ★
penisu
ペニス

Head ★
kitō
亀頭

The rim of the head ★
kari
カリ
Also the chin—basically another word for the head.

Balls (testicles) ★★★
kintama
金玉

Nuts ★★
tamatama
たまたま

Pubic hair (male) ★★
chinge
チン毛

Tits ★★★
oppai
おっぱい

Can you touch my tits?
watashi no oppai sawatte kureru
私のおっぱい触ってくれる?

Nipples ★★★
chikubi
乳首

Nips ★
bī chiku
ビーチク

Pussy ★★★
manko
マンコ

Pubic hair (female) ★★
mange
まん毛

Shaved pussy ★★★
paipan
パイパン

Clit ★★★
kuri
クリ

G-spot ★★
jī supo
Gスポ

Pussy lips ★★
bira bira
ビラビラ

Ass ★★★
ketsu
ケツ

Asshole ★★
ketsu ana
ケツ穴

Anus ★★★
anaru
アナル

Sperm ★★★
seieki
精液

Pussy juice ★★
aieki
愛液

Big dick ★★★
dekachin
デカチン

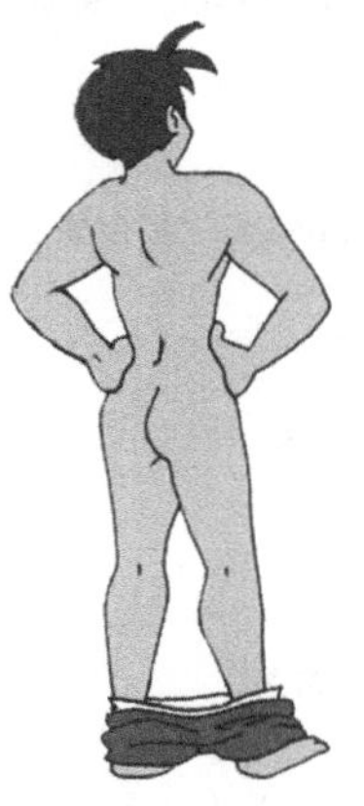

Limp dick ★★★
fu'nyachin
フニャチン

Hard dick ★★
katai chinko
硬いちんこ

Soft dick ★★
yawarakai chinko
柔らかいちんこ

Shabby-looking dick ★★★
sochin
粗チン

•••••Dirty Japanese

kitanai nihongo

汚い日本語

Personally, I hate this section the most, LOL. I think some people will find it disgusting, so read only the parts you need.

Piss ★★
shonben
しょんべん

I wanna go pee. ★★★
oshikko shitai
おしっこしたい。

I gotta take a leak. ★★
shonben shitai
小便したい。

Lets piss together! ★★
tsureshon *shiyo!*
連れションしよ!

I wet the bed. ★★
onesho shichatta
おねしょしちゃった。

Look! That drunk guy is pissing in public! ★★
Mite ano yopparai no otoko ga ***tasshon*** *shiteru!*
見て!あの酔っぱらいの男が立っしょんしてる!

Shit ★★★
kuso
くそ
The word "くそ (*kuso*: shit)" is used in a variety of situations. Basically, it is used in the same way as the English word "shit": when you have made a mistake, or are frustrated, or just swearing. It is not often used as a word for excrement.

I need to poop. ★★
unko *shitai*
うんこしたい。

I gotta take a dump. ★
kuso *shitai*
くそしたい。

I've got nasty diarrhea. ★★
yabai geri shiteru
ヤバいゲリしてる。

I've been super constipated lately. ★★★
saikin wa meccha ***benpi*** *nanda*
最近はめっちゃ便秘なんだ。

Watch out! There's poop over there! ★★★
ki o tsukete! soko ni unchi aruyo
気をつけて！そこにうんちあるよ！
(more casual than うんこ)

Farts ★★★
onara
おなら

Who farted! ★★★
onara shita *no wa doitsu da*
オナラしたのはどいつだ！

Why do I so relish the smell of my own farts? ★★
jibun no onara no ***nioi*** *ga kon'nanimo konomashī no wa naze darō*
自分のオナラの臭いがこんなにも好ましいのはなぜだろう？

Were you pulling some nasty silent farts? ★★
kimi ***sukashippe*** *shita*
君、すかしっ屁した？
The word "sukashippe"（すかしっ屁）literally means "transparent fart," and roughly corresponds to the English "silent-but-deadly."

And for your present I got you . . . a cup of tea! ★
hai kimi no purezento wa ***nigirippe*** *da*
はい、君のプレゼントは . . . にぎりっ屁だ！
The meaning of "*nigirippe*（にぎりっ屁）" is to hold a fart in your hand, bring it close to your friend's nose, and then spread your fingers.

Snot / boogers ★★
hanamizu / hanakuso
鼻水 / 鼻くそ

Hey, stop picking your nose. ★★
kora ***hana hojiru*** *na*
こら、鼻ほじるな。

Dude, don't wipe your boogers on me! ★★
oi jibun no ***hanakuso*** *o boku ni tsukeru na yo*
おい、自分の鼻くそを僕につけるなよ！

You got a tissue? ★★★
tisshu *aru*
ティッシュある？

I've got a bloody nose. ★★★
hanaji *ga deta*
鼻血が出た。

You've got eye boogers. ★★
meyani *ga tsuiteruyo*
目ヤニがついてるよ。

Shit, I got a zit on my face. ★★★
kuso kao ni ***nikibi*** *ga dekita*
くそ、顔にニキビができた。

I could hear that person snoring from outside! ★★
ano hito no ***ibiki*** *ga soto kara kikoerun*
あの人のイビキが外から聞こえる！

She grinds her teeth like crazy. ★★
kanojo wa hidoi ***hagishiri*** *surun dayo*
彼女はひどい歯ぎしりするんだよ。

••••••Sickness
byōki
病気

Sickness ★★★
byōki
病気

My mother has a mental sickness.
watashi no haha wa, seishin no byōki wo motteiru
私の母は、精神の病気を持っている。

You all right? ★★★
daijōbu *kai*
大丈夫かい?

I'm not feeling good lately. ★★★
saikin wa ***taichō ga yokunai***
最近は体調がよくない.

I feel gross. ★★★
kimochi warui
気持ち悪い。

I feel nauseous. ★★★
hakike *ga suru*
吐き気がする。

I think I caught a cold. ★★★
kaze *o hīta mitai*
風邪を引いたみたい。

I've got a **headache.** ★★★
zutsū *ga suru*
頭痛がする。

I've got a **stomachache.** ★★★
fukutsuu *ga suru*
腹痛がする。

Call a **doctor.** ★★★
isha *o yonde*
医者を呼んで。

Get me some **painkiller,** please. ★★★
itamidome *o kudasai*
痛み止めをください。

I'm having my **period.** ★★★
ima wa ***seirichū*** *nano*
今は生理中なの。

I have pretty **heavy periods.** ★★★
atashi wa ***seiri ga omoi****nda,*
あたしは生理が重いんだ。

I'm all **hung over** today. ★★★
kyō wa ***futsukayoi*** *nanda*
今日は二日酔いなんだ。

My friend with benefits gave me **gonorrhea.** ★
sefure ni ***rimbyō*** *o moratcchatta*
セフレに淋病をもらっちゃった。

Chlamydia is difficult to notice. ★
kuramijia *wa kidzuki nikui*
クラミジアは気付きにくい。

CHAPTER 7

HORNY JAPANESE

MURAMURA NIHONGO

ムラムラ日本語

To be honest, there are quite a few radical things in this chapter. Of course, the content is something you would never find in a textbook. For this chapter, I relied not only on my own knowledge, but also on the internet, and I even asked some of my friends to check the information to make sure it was accurate. And I included words I have heard many times in my life.

To those who are not comfortable with graphic erotic language, I recommend that they refrain from reading this chapter. However, I would like people who are passionate about learning to give it a try.

•••••Affirmative consent

sekkyoku teki doui

積極的同意

Consent for sexual activity in Japan is based on "affirmative consent," as in the US and other countries. In other words, ask your partner and get their permission before touching or inserting. You can use these phrases to help check consent.

What feels good to you? ★★★
doushitara kimochi ii
どうしたら気持ちいい?

Can I touch your . . .? ★★★
. . . sawatte mo ī
. . .触ってもいい?

LOVE HOTEL

RABU HOTERU

ラブホテル

In Japan, there are love hotels where you can use a room for a short time for sex. So, if you don't want to go all the way to your lover's house, you can pay to use a nearby love hotel. There are two main plans at love hotels—"rest" and "stay." For a "rest" you can expect to pay around 6,000 to 8,000 yen for three hours, and for an overnight "stay," you can expect to pay around 13,000 to 17,000 yen from 8 p.m. to 10 a.m. the next morning. The price is not per person; you only pay for the room. However, usually no more than two people can stay in the room. If there are three or more people, it will either be prohibited, or you will need to pay an additional fee.

Condoms, lotion, and other items are available in the hotel for use at any time. Using love hotels is common, and not just for people with unusual sexual preferences or suspicious relationships—university students and married couples also use them casually. Most of the people I know have used them at least once. There are also many clean love hotels where you can enjoy Netflix, games, and karaoke. So, these days, some girls go to love hotels with their friends just to have a regular party.

Can I touch you here? (pointing to body part) ★★★
koko sawatte iiyo
ここ触っていいよ?

Do you want me to keep going? ★★★
tsudzukete hoshii
続けて欲しい?

Yes, don't stop. ★★★
un, yamenaide
うん、やめないで。

How far can we go? ★★★
dokomade dekiru
どこまでできる?

We can do everything. ★★★
zenbu iiyo
全部いいよ。

Do you want more? ★★★
motto hoshii
もっと欲しい?

What do you want me to do? ★★★
nani wo shite hoshii
何をしてほしい?

That's all for now. ★★★
kokomade de owari ne
ここまでで終わりね。

Do you want me to stop? ★★★
yamete hoshi i
やめて欲しい?

Please don't do this. ★★★
kore wa yamete ne
これはやめてね。

Do you want a minute to think? ★★★
sukoshi kangaeru jikan hoshii
少し考える時間欲しい?

Touch my . . . ★★★
. . . sawatte
. . .触って。

Lick my . . . ★★★
. . . namete
. . .なめて。

Japanese men don't generally slap women on the bottom, so it's necessary to ask first!

Spank my . . . ★
. . . tataite
. . .叩いて。

Be gentle with my . . . ★★
. . . teinei ni atsukatte
. . .丁寧に扱って。

I'm getting in the mood to . . . ★★★
. . . ki ni natte kita
. . .気になってきた。

Let's go home and . . . ★★★
ie ni kaette . . . koto ni shiyō
家に帰って. . .ことにしよう。

How 'bout we . . . ★★★
. . . no wa dō
. . .のはどう?

You probably won't be asked directly to have sex. Of course, it's ideal to ask for permission directly, but sometimes it's implied, like in the expression "Netflix and chill," so here I'll introduce some phrases that could indicate indirectly that the other person wants to have sex. These phrases don't guarantee that the person definitely wants to have sex, but it's very useful to understand the sentences that could indicate the unspoken expectation.

Let's take a break. ★★★

kyuukei shiyou

休憩しよう。

In this case, there is a fairly high probability that they are going to have sex at home or in a love hotel. So, if you hear this phrase, you should know it's very likely that they want to have sex with you. On the other hand, if you want to initiate, you can start the conversation by saying something like this:

> **I'm getting tired**
>
> *nanka tsukarete kita*
>
> なんか疲れてきた
>
> This phrase will then lead the conversation naturally to:
>
> **Shall we take a break?**
>
> *jaa kyuukei suru*
>
> じゃあ休憩する?

Even if the last train has gone, it's okay. ★★★

shuuden nakunattemo daijoubu dayo.

終電なくなっても大丈夫だよ

What this means is that even if you miss the last train and can't go home, you can stay at the other person's house. Since you are staying at the other person's house, there is a high possibility they are expecting sex.

Are you busy tomorrow morning? ★★★

ashita asa isogashii

明日朝忙しい?

This question suggests there's a possibility you will be able to stay at the other person's house overnight. If a woman asks, it gives the impression she is inviting the gentleman to her house for the night.

Want to have a drink at my place? 

uchi de nomanai

うちで飲まない?

A man may also use the excuse of drinking alcohol to invite a woman to his house. Of course, if they are alone together, the other person is expecting sex. However, since they are both drinking alcohol, it is also a situation where misunderstandings are likely to occur, so it is even more important to have affirmative consent.

••••••Fucking
ecchi
エッチ

Pornography ★★★
ero
エロ

> **Pornography and art are similar.**
> ***ero** to āto wa nite imasu*
> エロとアートは似ています。

Erotic ★★★
eroi
エロい

> **My girlfriend is erotic** (sexy).
> *boku no kanojo wa **eroi***
> 僕の彼女はエロい。

Get it on ★★★
ecchi suru
エッチする

> **Hey, let's get it on.**
> *nene, ecchi shiyou*
> ねね、エッチしよう。

Sex (a little formal) ★★
sekkusu
セックス

> **I can't have sex tonight.**
> *konya wa* **sekkusu** *deki nai.*
> 今夜はセックスできない。

Fuck (dirty Japanese) ★★★
yaru
やる

I really wanna fuck.
hontou ni ***yaritai***
本当にやりたい

Fuck like rabbits ★★
yarimakuru
やりまくる

Sex-obsessed club ★★
yarisā
ヤリサー

There is a term "ヤリサー (*yarisā*: sex-obsessed club)." At Japanese universities, there are clubs that might be called tennis clubs, etc., but that in reality are groups of people who have sex together on a regular basis. I don't know if these really exist, but everyone knows the phrase.

Have a quickie ★
ippatsu kamasu
一発かます

Tap that and/or bone ★★
hameru
ハメる

Photographing or filming sex ★★
hame dori
ハメ撮り

……Coming

iku

イク

When written in katakana, the word "イク(*iku*: coming)" has a 99 percent erotic meaning. So be careful. When written in hiragana, it depends on the context. For example, the sentence "一人でいくね (*hitori de iku ne*: I'm going alone)" would mean you are going somewhere alone, unless it is used in an erotic context. However, if I received a message saying "一人でイクね (*hitori de iku ne*: I'm coming alone)," I would probably spit my coffee out. No matter how accurate the context is, we'll still spend at least a second wondering whether it has an erotic meaning or not. With other words, it doesn't really matter whether you write them in hiragana or katakana, but with this word, the meaning can be very different.

Orgasming (guys, girls) ★★★
iku
イク

Leaking / coming out ★★
deru
出る

Ugh . . . my sperm is about to come out.
yabai... sorosoro desou
やばい、、、そろそろでそう。

Ejaculation (formal) ★
shasei
射精

A wet dream ★
musei
夢精

Erect ★★★
tatsu
立つ
Literally, "standing up" penis.

Since "ちんこ: dick" is considered vulgar, we often say things like:

My thing is gradually standing up.
boku no asoko ga tatte kita
僕のあそこが立ってきた。

Or we don't say the subject and just say:

Hard ★★★
katai
硬い

It's getting hard.
kataku natte kita
硬くなってきた。

Erection ★★
bokki
勃起

Foreplay ★★★
zengi
前戯

Sex without foreplay is not sex.
zengi ga nai sekkusu wa, sekkusu dewa nai
前戯がないセックスは、セックスではない。

Feather touch ★★
fezā tacchi
フェザータッチ

Useful Phrases

I want to come. ★★
ikitai
イキたい。

I'm about to come. ★★★
ikisō
イキそう。

I'm coming! ★★★
iku iku
イクイク!

Where do you want it? ★★
doko ni hoshī
どこに欲しい?

I just came. ★★★
itchatta
イっちゃった。

Do you have a . . .? ★★★
. . . aru
. . .ある?

Do you have a condom?
kondōmu aru
コンドームある?

Let's try using a . . . ★★★
. . . tsukatte miyō ka
. . .使ってみようか?

••••••Sexual acts
seikōi
性行為

Let's first learn the vocabulary, then commonly used phrases.

Condom ★★★
kondōmu
コンドーム

Raw (sex without using a condom) ★★★
nama
生

I'm a little scared to do it raw.
***nama** de suruno wa chotto kowai na*
生でするのはちょっと怖いな。

Ejaculating (coming) **inside** ★★★
nakadashi
中出し

If you're going to come inside me, you'd better take responsibility.
***nakadashi** surunara sekinin totte yo ne*
中出しするなら責任とってよね。

Petting ★★
*atama **pon pon** suru*
頭ポンポンする

Blow job ★★★
fera
フェラ

Fellatio ★★
ferachio
フェラチオ

Playing the skin flute ★
shakuhachi
尺八

Swallowing ★★
gokkun
ごっくん

Eating out ★★★
kunni
クンニ

Cunnilingus ★
kunniringusu
クンニリングス

Sixty-nine ★★★
shikkusu nain
シックスナイン

G-spot ★★
gī supotto
Gスポット

Female ejaculation ★★
shio fuki
潮吹き

Fingering ★★
te man
手マン

Tits job ★★
pai zuri
パイズリ
Pai means "おっぱい: tits" and *zuri* means "こする: scrub"

••••••More specialized adult words
yori senmontekina adarutona kotoba
より専門的なアダルトな言葉

Missionary position ★★★
seijōi
正常位

Doggy-style ★★★
bakku
バック

Woman on top ★★★
kijōi
騎乗位

Sitting on face ★★
gammen kijō
顔面騎乗

Hard fucking ★
pisuton undō
ピストン運動
Literally, "piston motion."

Threesome ★★
sanpī
3ピー

Orgy ★
rankō
乱交

Post-nut clarity (guy's change in mood/personality after coming) ★★
kenja taimu
賢者タイム

Facial (formal) ★★
gansha
顔射

Facial ★★
bukkake
ぶっかけ
This is a more informal term than *gansha*.

Premature ejaculation ★★
sōrō
早漏

Delayed ejaculation ★★
chirō
遅漏

Viagra ★★
baiagura
バイアグラ

Lotion ★★★
rōsh on
ローション

Do you have any lotion?
***rōshon** o motte imasu ka?*
ローションを持っていますか?

•••••Unusual words in Japan
nihon no kawatta kotoba
日本の変わった言葉

Tuna ★★
maguro
マグロ
In Japan, a person who is always passive and doesn't move at all during sex is called a "マグロ (*maguro*: tuna)." At first glance, this term seems contradictory, because a tuna fish will die if it stops swimming. However, the meaning of tuna here is frozen tuna. A person who doesn't make a sound, doesn't react at all, and just lies there during sex is called (frozen) tuna, but nowadays the term "tuna" is used in a broader sense to refer to a person who doesn't move during sex.

The 48 basic sexual positions ★
shijuu hatte
48手
There are many different sexual positions, but in Japan it is said that there are 48 of them.

Useful phrases

I want to do some . . . ★★★
. . . ga shitai
. . .がしたい。

I want to kiss you!
anata to kisu ga shitai
あなたとキスがしたい！

Do you wanna try . . .? ★★★
. . . yatte mitai
. . .やってみたい？

Do you want to try the 48 basic sexual positions together?
issho ni shijuu hatte yatte mitai
一緒に48手やってみたい？

Have you ever done . . .? ★★★
. . . shita koto aru
. . .したことある？

Have you ever had sex?
sekkusu shitakoto aru
セックスしたことある？

I like . . . ★★★
. . . ga suki
. . .が好き。

I like doggy-style.
watashi wa bakku ga suki
私はバックが好き。

I'm getting tired of . . . ★★
. . . akite kita
. . .飽きてきた。

I'm getting tired of the missionary position.
seijōi ni akite kita
正常位に飽きてきた。

Do it . . . ★★★
shite . . .
して. . .

Do it now.
mou shite
もうして。

. . . faster. ★★★
. . . hayaku
. . .速く

Go faster.
hayaku ugoite
速く動いて。

. . . slower. ★★★
. . . yukkuri
. . .ゆっくり

Touch me slower.
yukkuri sawatte
ゆっくり触って。

. . . harder. ★★
. . . hageshiku
. . .激しく

Do it harder!
hageshiku shite
激しくして!

. . . softer. ★★★
. . . yasashiku
. . .やさしく

Kiss me softer.
yasashiku kisu shite
やさしくキスして。

. . . more. ★★★
. . . motto
. . .もっと

I wanna do more.
motto shitai
もっとしたい。

That feels really good! ★★★
meccha kimochi ī
めっちゃ気持ちいい！

That hurts a little. ★★★
chotto itai
ちょっと痛い。

I'm starting to get off. ★★★
kimochi yoku nattekita
気持ちよくなってきた。

•••••Porn
poruno
ポルノ

Porn is very popular, and the industry is thriving. You'll find many different kinds of porn; some are even technically illegal in Japan. For example, it is illegal to upload uncensored videos so when you are in Japan, make sure you use a mosaic or blurring effect if you upload your homemade videos to the internet.

Pornhub is famous in Japan as well as in other countries. For a while, there was a commercial on Pornhub that started with the line "Hey guys we have a gift for you." One year there was a Japanese news article about how an English sentence that started with "Hey guys," given in a university-entrance exam taken by all Japanese high-school students, prevented the male students from concentrating on the exam. Pornhub is that famous. There is also another very popular adult video company in Japan, despite the fact it charges for its content; it's called FANZA. The quality of the videos, the actresses, the situations, everything, is of a very high standard, and many Japanese people know about it.

Porn (official) ★
poruno
ポルノ

Erotic videos ★★★
ero bideo
エロ動画

Porn videos ★★★
ēbui
AV
アダルトビデオ: adult video. To be honest, there are countless genres of pornographic videos. Here, I will list those that relatively many people have heard of. Sorry if your favorite genre is not on the list!

Western-style ★★
youmono
洋もの

Student ★★
gakusei
学生

Amateur ★★★
shirouto
素人

Clean-style / Refined ★★★
seiso
清楚

Fantasy ★★
fantajī
ファンタジー

Cuckold ★★
netorare
ネトラレ
Pr, using Romaji, "NTR."

Swapping ★
suwappingu
スワッピング

First sexual experience ★★★
hatsu taiken
初体験

Incest ★★
kinshin soukan
近親相姦

Freezing animation ★
jikan teishi
時間停止

Hole brothers (guys who had sex with the same girl in the past) ★★
ana kyoudai
穴兄弟

Penis sisters (girls who had sex with the same guy in the past) ★
saoshimai
竿姉妹

•••••Masturbation

onanī
オナニー

Masturbation was once considered something shameful. It was unthinkable for a woman to talk about masturbating. However, that is not the case at all now. While many Japanese women won't say up front that they masturbate on their own initiative, there is nothing shameful about saying they do, if asked at the right time. It means we all have sexual desires, and there is no need to hide them, because having them is normal. Recently, many tools have been developed to help both men and women masturbate. Here, are some of the more common ones.

Fap (noun) ★★★
onanī
オナニー

Fap (verb) ★★★
onaru
オナる

Jerk off ★★
shikoru
シコる

Masturbation (formal, Japanese) ★
jii koui
自慰行為

Masturbation (formal, foreign word) ★
masutā bē syon
マスターベーション

Pleasuring yourself (mostly for girls, formal) ★
serufu prejā
セルフプレジャー
Used by women who are embarrassed to say the word "masturbation" directly.

Nofap ★★★
ona kin
オナ禁

TENGA ★★
tenga
テンガ
The most famous company for male masturbation devices in Japan.

Hand job ★★★
tekoki
手コキ

Finger-banging ★★★
teman
手マン

Masturbation device that simulates female genitalia ★★★
onaho
オナホ
オナニーホール (masturbation hole)

Love doll ★
rabu dōru
ラブドール

Vibrator (vibe) ★★★
baibu
バイブ

Dildo ★★
dirudo
ディルド

Bullet (egg) **vibrator** ★★
pinku rōta
ピンクローター

Penis band ★
peniban
ペニバン

••••• Prostitution

fūzoku

風俗

It is illegal to have vaginal sex for money in Japan so sex establishments only offer hand jobs, blow jobs, etc.

But where there is a will, there is a way. Take the establishment called a soapland. You pay a hefty entrance fee (much higher that a regular bathhouse). However, when you go to the designated bath, by chance you may encounter a woman there and fall in love. As a result, you can have sex. The logic of these shops is that since free love is not illegal under the law, this is not illegal.

This may sound ridiculous, but soaplands are very common. It's not illegal, and they operate out in the open. The police know about these incredibly lucky encounters but don't really crack down on soaplands.

If you're a visitor to Japan and want to use adult services, you should be careful: Many places will not accept foreigners because of past problems. Some girls are afraid of doing sexual things with someone they can't clearly communicate with and who is physically large and could potentially dominate or possibly harm them. Even if you are allowed to use these services, the price may be higher for you than for Japanese customers. There are also many fake shops where even if you ask for a beautiful girl, you may actually end up with someone you are not happy with, so it may be difficult to find a satisfactory service on your own. So, using adult establishments in Japan is not recommended; but there are plenty of great adult toys and videos you can enjoy.

Japanese products are famous for their high quality. Japanese food is delicious because it is made with the utmost attention to details, pleasing to all the senses. Likewise, adult toys are made with similar care—they are designed to be warm to the touch and feel good to the skin; there is also a lot of research behind the frequency and intensity of toys that vibrate.

Adult videos are also made with the same attention to detail, making them exciting and using the most advanced camera technology to make the videos feel as real and raw as possible.

Prostitution ★★★
fūzoku
風俗

Escort service ★★
deriheru
デリヘル

Brothel where one can bathe with the prostitutes ★★
sōpu / "sōpurando"
ソープ / ソープランド

Hand job ★★
tekoki
手コキ

Prostitution in which services are provided by several women in rotation ★★
pinsaro
ピンサロ

When people think of the sex industry, the first thing that many people imagine is a call girl. Below are some words related to call girls—the content is quite geeky, so you can skip it if you like. I've done my best to make sure the information is as accurate as possible, but there may be some slight inaccuracies.

I will first introduce the "basic sex play," but of course the meaning of this will differ depending on the store.

Basic sex play ★★★
kihon purei
基本プレイ

Blow job without a condom ★★★
nama fera
生フェラ

Grinding (without inserting) ★★★
sumata
素股

Ball licking ★★
tama name
玉舐め

Full-body lip service ★
zenshin rippu
全身リップ

Verbal abuse ★★
kotoba zeme
言葉責め

Finger insertion ★
yubi ire
指入れ

From here on, there are many things you can do, for an additional fee, in addition to the basic play.

Optional play ★★★
opushon purei
オプションプレイ

Blindfold ★★★
ai masuku
アイマスク

Hand and foot restraints, handcuffs ★★★
tekase, ashikase, tejou
手枷、足枷、手錠

No panties, no bra ★★★
nō pan, nō bura
ノーパン、ノーブラ

Pantyhose ★★
pansuto
パンスト

Take girl's pants home with you ★
pantsu omochi kaeri
パンツお持ち帰り

Fishnet tights ★★
ami taitsu
網タイツ

Stocking-ripping ★
pansuto yaburi
パンスト破り

Watching girl's masturbation ★
onani kanshou
オナニー鑑賞

Electric massage wand ★★★
denma
電マ

Blow job immediately once a girl gets inside of your room ★★
soku shayku
即尺

Swallowing ★★
gokkun
ごっくん

Rim job ★★
anaru name
アナル舐め

Prostate massage ★
zenritsusen massāji
前立腺マッサージ

Filming video ★★★
douga satsuei
動画撮影

Anal fuck ★★
ēefu
AF
For some reason, paying for vaginal sex is illegal, but paying for anal sex is not illegal. Japanese laws are complicated.

All the way (have sex; only in prostitution) ★★★
honban
本番

> **I hear that girl would go all the way.**
> *anoko wa honban dekiru rashii yo*
> あの子は本番できるらしいよ。

A girl who will have sex in a brothel although it's illegal ★
kiban
基盤

> **This girl (in a brothel) is one who will have sex.**
> *konoko wa **kiban** dayo*
> この子は基盤だよ。

A girl who will have sex for money in a brothel secretly ★
enban
円盤

That is a girl who will have sex with you for an additional fee.
ano ko wa kiban dakedo ***enban*** *da yo*
あの子は基盤だけど円盤だよ。

"Behind the scenes" options ★
ura opu
裏オプ

Photoshopped ★★
pane maji
パネまじ
Literally "panel magic."

•••••Cosplay
kosupure
コスプレ

Cosplay is a big business in Japan. It' no surprise that people bring their hobbies into the bedroom. Here are some costumes people choose to wear; outfits can also be purchased or rented at love hotels.

Sailor suit / school uniform ★★★
sērā fuku / seifuku
セーラー服 / 制服

Anime ★★★
anime
アニメ

Nurse ★★★
nāsu
ナース

Gym shorts ★★★
taisou fuku
体操服

Suit ★
sūtu
スーツ

Female teacher ★★
josei kyoushi
女性教師

Maid costume ★★★
meido fuku
メイド服

Chinese dress ★★★
chaina fuku
チャイナ服

CA (cabin attendant) ★★★
shī ē
CA

Naked Y-shirt (a girl wearing a man's button-up shirt without a bra) ★
hadaka wai shatsu
裸Yシャツ

Naked apron ★
hadaka epuron
裸エプロン

Paddock Girls ★
rēsu kuīn
レースクイーン

Prostitutes for women

Until now, prostitution has always been associated with men, but recently, prostitution for women has become more popular. It is used by women who are tired of men who only have sex at their own convenience. Its explosive rise in popularity was due to the fact that even celebrities use it. Of course, there are also various brothels specializing in gay and lesbian customers.

•••••Prostitution via apps
apuri deno baisyun
アプリでの売春

There are women who use apps to privately offer prostitution services, but this is a crime in Japan, and you should never use these services. There is a real risk of being caught by the police; there is also the possibility of being scammed in a fake prostitution sting. If you use a brothel, there is a certain level of safety guaranteed, but if you are doing it privately, you never know what might happen. Even if you get scammed, of course you can't go to the police, since you yourself are committing a crime in the first place. Here I will introduce some of the words commonly used in prostitution on such apps. This is because you may end up committing this type of crime without even knowing it, being forced to pay money under the name of "date expenses."

Turn tricks ★★★
enkou
援交
Since "援交: *enkou*" is illegal, people deliberately use different kanji to write it, such as 円光 (*enkou*), 縁光 (*enkou*), etc. I'm going

to say it again: **This is a serious crime, so you mustn't use these.**

15,000 yen [$100 US dollars in 2024] hotel not included ★★★
hobetsu ichigo
ホ別いちご

The word "ホ別 (*hobetsu*)" stands for "ホテル代別 (*hoterudai betsu*: it doesn't include the hotel fee)." The word "いちご (*ichigo*: strawberry)" can be read as 1 (*ichi*) or 5 (*go*) in Japanese, so instead of 15,000 yen, the secret word *ichigo* is used. This is to avoid detection by the police.

> **To meet me, please pay 15,000 yen; hotel not included.**
> *watashi to au niwa hobetu ichigo de onegai shimasu*
> 私と会うにはホ別いちごでお願いします。

SUGAR DADDIES

PAPA KATSU

パパ活

Recently, the term "パパ活 (*papa katsu*: having a sugar daddy)" has become popular and has even been reported in the news. パパ (papa) usually means "father" but here means a patron who will give you money. You can get around 10,000 yen ($64 US dollars in 2024) for an hour of tea at a cafe. Of course, some people here also have sex for more money. However, the term "papa katsu" is recognized as basically being a healthy dating service, as opposed to a sex service, so people who privately offer prostitution services are also starting to use the term. I haven't heard much about it, but it seems that "ママ活 (*mama katsu*: having a sugar mama)" also exists.

Including sex ★★★
otona ari
大人あり

This dating includes sex.
kono dēto wa otona ari desu
このデートは大人ありです。

In car (car sex, etc.) ★★
shanai
車内

It's 5,000 yen in car.
shanai wa go sen en desu
車内は5000円です。

For sex ★★★
yari moku
やりもく

I'm not here for sex.
yari moku *okotowari*
やりもくお断り。

For free food ★★★
meshi moku
飯もく

She pretends to be interested, but all she wants is to eat for free.
ki ga aru furi shiteiru kedo anoko wa ***meshi moku*** *na dake*
気があるふりしているけどあの子は飯もくなだけ。

A badger game (acting as if you are having an affair for blackmail) ★★★
tsutsumotase
美人局

••••••Sadomasochism (S&M)

esuemu

SM

The most important thing in S&M is the relationship of mutual trust. Sadists and masochists can only focus on pleasure in a safe environment.

Sadomasochism (S&M) ★★★
esuemu
SM

Sadist ★★★
esu
S

Masochist ★★★
emu
M

Mistress ★★★
jouōsama
女王様
A term used to refer to a woman who is dominant in S&M play. She is often seen wearing fishnet tights, high heels, and carrying a whip.

Training ★★★
choukyou
調教
Originally a word used to describe disciplining animals such as horses, but it is also used to educate people according to their tastes and to bring out their untapped sexual preferences.

Pig ★★
butayarou
豚野郎
A term used by a dominatrix to verbally abuse a man, and also a term used to refer to a man.

Whip ★★★
muti
鞭
A tool used by the mistress to beat the "pig."

Candles ★★★
kyandoru
キャンドル
Used in S&M, but designed so they do not burn.

Soft play ★★
sofuto purei
ソフトプレイ
Does not involve a lot of pain, though what "soft play" means exactly will vary from person to person.

Abnormal play ★★
abunōmaru purei
アブノーマルプレイ
A special kind of play that is particularly unique to each person. We each have our own preferred fantasies when it comes to sex. For example, your strict boss may be a baby and make sweet noises when having sex. The play I am about to describe is an abnormal play that you may hear about relatively often.

Voyeurism ★
shikan
視姦
Means humiliating someone by watching them.

Spanking ★★★
spankingu
スパンキング
Play in which the buttocks are spanked.

Full-body service ★★★
zenshin houshi
全身奉仕
Refers to a woman using her hands or mouth to torment a man's genitals.

Shame play ★
shuuchi purei
羞恥プレイ
Involves making a person feel ashamed, saying or making them say embarrassing things, or otherwise stimulating their sense of shame.

Cross-dressing ★
josou purei
女装プレイ
Where a man wears makeup and women's clothes and underwear.

Infantile play ★
youji purei
幼児プレイ
In which a man mainly acts as an infant. It's also called 赤ちゃんプレイ (*akatyan purei*: baby play).

Scatology ★
sukatoro purei / golden purei
スカトロプレイ / 黄金プレイ
Play in which sexual arousal is experienced through excrement such as urine, feces, and vomit, and in which these are used. It's also called 黄金プレイ (*ougon purei*: golden play).

Vomiting play ★
ōto purei
嘔吐プレイ
In which a person vomits up what they have eaten.

Holy water play ★
seisui purei
聖水プレイ
In which a man drinks or is sprayed with a woman's urine.

Outdoor play ★★
yagai purei
野外プレイ
Is sexual play that takes place outdoors, such as in a park. (In Japan, this is a crime.)

NG play ★★★
enujī purei
NGプレイ
Is play that cannot be practiced for various reasons, such as the partner does not want to do it or it is not legal.

CHAPTER 8

SEXY ONOMATOPOEIA

SEKUSHĪ NA ONOMATOPE

セクシーなオノマトペ

In this chapter, we will study sexy onomatopoeia. You will probably be surprised by how much of this there is in Japanese. In fact, Japanese has a huge number of onomatopoetic expressions and words that imitate sensations and sounds. Onomatopoetic words are directly linked to our senses, so if you can master them, you can use the language more, as Japanese people do. They are useful above all because you can use them in many different situations. This is another reason why my YouTube channel, Onomappu, teaches Japanese with a focus on onomatopoeia.

It isn't possible to translate all onomatopoetic Japanese words into English, of course, but I'll explain each "dirty Japanese" onomatopoetic word introduced here. One thing to know is that the meanings of these words are the same whether written in hiragana or in katakana.

nuru nuru ★★★

ぬるぬる

The lubricant-like fluid that comes from a woman's vagina. You can say this word with an innocent look on your face.

> **Why is it so *nuru nuru* here?**
> *koko wa konna ni* ***nuru nuru*** *shiteiru no*
> ここはこんなにぬるぬるしているの?

nume nume ★

ぬめぬめ

This word is like "ぬるぬる (*nuru nuru*)" but contains slightly unpleasant overtones. So you can say things like this:

> **This fork is slimy like *nume nume*. Did you wash it well?**
> *Kono fōku wa numenume shite iru. Yoku aratta?*
> このフォークはぬめぬめしている。よく洗った?

kuchu kuchu ★★

くちゅくちゅ

This is often used when describing the sound that is heard inside a woman's vagina.

> **I get excited when I hear that *kuchu kuchu* sound.**
> *boku wa ano* ***kuchu kuchu*** *to iu oto o kiku to koufun surunda*
> 僕はあのくちゅくちゅという音を聞くと興奮するんだ。

jupu jupu ★

じゅぷじゅぷ

A slightly lower-pitched sound than the "kuchu kuchu" sound. This is the sound you hear when you're having sex with a very wet woman.

> **You must have been wet, because I could hear *jupu jupu*.**
> ***jupu jupu*** *tte iu oto ga kikoetashi, nureteirun desho*
> じゅぷじゅぷっていう音が聞こえたし、濡れているんでしょ。

juru juru ★★
じゅるじゅる

This is the sound of sucking something with a slightly viscous consistency. When you're hungry and your drool is about to drip, you make this sound when you suck it up in a hurry. However, during sex, the woman's fluids are overflowing, and the sound changes to that of sucking them up.

> **I'll suck it all up like *juru juru*.**
> ***juru juru*** *subete sui tsukusu yo*
> じゅるじゅる全て吸い尽くすよ。

gusho gusho ★★
ぐしょぐしょ

Describes the appearance of pants or sheets that are wet with liquid.

> **Your pants are all wet like *gusho gusho*, what were you thinking?**
> *pantsu ga* ***gusho gusho*** *ni nurete iruyo, nani o kangaeteru no*
> パンツがぐしょぐしょに濡れているよ、何を考えてるの?

zubo zubo ★★
ずぼずぼ

The sound of a penis being inserted and removed during sex. Here, it expresses the appearance of something large entering. If you want to emphasize the overflowing of liquid, I think the *jupu jupu* we learned earlier is good.

> **It's going in and out of me like *zubo zubo!***
> *watashi no naka o* ***zubo zubo*** *to detari haittari shiteru*
> 私の中をずぼずぼと出たり入ったりしてる!

an an ★★★
アンアン

A moan. I think the way people moan differs from country to country, but many Japanese people moan *an an*.

If you moan that loudly, people outside will hear you saying *an an*!
*sonnani ookina koe de aeidara, soto no hito ni **an an** itteiru noga kikoechau*
そんなに大きな声で喘いだら、外の人にアンアン言っているのが聞こえちゃう!

pero pero ★★★
ぺろぺろ
Means to lick using the tongue. It expresses the way a small tongue moves. It is commonly used in phrases like "licking candy," but when used like this, the meaning changes.

Can I lick your dick like *pero pero*?
*ochinchin o **pero pero** shitemo ii*
おちんちんをぺろぺろしてもいい?

rero rero ★
れろれろ
The word *rero rero* gives the image of someone kneading a candy with their tongue.

Don't lick my nipples like *rero rero*.
*chikubi o **rero rero** namenaide*
乳首をれろれろ舐めないで。

mura mura ★★★
ムラムラ
In English, this is called "horny."

Your body is so sexy that I'm getting *mura mura.*
*kimi no karada ga sekushii de **mura mura** shitekita*
君の体がセクシーでムラムラしてきた。

shiko shiko ★★
しこしこ
Describes the motion of a hand stroking a dick.

I'm so horny, I want to stroke it like *shiko shiko*.
*sugoku mura mura shitete, **shiko shiko** shitai*
すごくムラムラしてて、しこしこしたい。

mokkori ★★

もっこり

This describes the appearance of an erection, especially when it can be seen through your clothes. If part of your trousers are tented, that's a *mokkori*.

> **Stay away from me! I'll get a hard-on like *mokkori*!**
> *oreni chidzukanaide!* ***mokkori*** *shichau*
> 俺に近づかないで!**もっこり**しちゃう!

muku muku ★

むくむく

The appearance of an erection.

> **Isn't it getting harder and harder like *muku muku*?**
> *nanka* ***muku muku*** *shitekite inai*
> なんか**むくむく**してきていない?

bin bin ★★★

びんびん

Describes a man's penis being very erect.

> **Oh my, you're already so hard like *bin bin*!**
> *ara, mou* ***bin bin*** *ni natteruwane*
> あら、もう**びんびん**になってるわね!

kachi kachi ★★★

カチカチ

Expresses the appearance of a man's penis being very hard.

> **I'd rather have a hard-on like *kachi kachi* than a limp one.**
> *watashi wa funya funya yorimo* ***kachi kachi*** *no hou ga suki*
> 私はフニャフニャよりも**カチカチ**の方が好き。

gin gin ★★

ギンギン

Expresses a man's penis being very hard and energetic.

It's so *gin gin* it looks like you could hammer a nail with it.
*kugi ga utesouna kurai sugoku **gin gin** ni natteiru yo*
釘が打てそうなくらいすごくギンギンになっているよ。

dopyu ★★
ドピュ
The sound of semen shooting out forcefully.

It came out so forcefully, like *dopyu*!
***dopyu** tto chikaraku detawane*
ドピュっと力強くでたわね!

iji iji ★
いじいじ
Playing with something by twisting it around with one's fingers.

You really like playing with your nipples like *iji iji*, don't you?
***iji iji** to chikubi o ijiru no ga sukinan desho*
いじいじと乳首を弄るのが好きなんでしょ?

gishi gishi ★★
ギシギシ
The sound of something creaking.

When I came home from work, I heard *gishi gishi* coming from the bedroom.
*shigoto kara kaeru to, shinshitsu kara **gishi gishi** to oto ga kikoeta*
仕事から帰ると、寝室からギシギシと音が聞こえた。

nettori ★★★
ねっとり
Having a sticky or slimy consistency.

I'll lick you up like *nettori*.
***nettori** namete ageru*
ねっとり舐めてあげる。

tapu tapu ★
たぷたぷ
The appearance of being full of liquid. When you have drunk a lot of water, you can say, "*おなかがたぷたぷだ* (*onaka ga tapu tapu da*: My stomach is so full)." You can sometimes say something like the following.

> **Your breasts are really big and floppy like *tapu tapu*.**
> *Kimi no mune wa hontōni ōkikute,* ***tapu tapu*** *shite iru*
> 君の胸は本当に大きくて、**たぷたぷ**している。

burun burun ★★
ぶるんぶるん
The appearance of something that sways due to vibration.

> **Look at that girl running. Her breasts are jiggling like *burun burun*.**
> *hashitte iru onnanoko o mite goran. Mune ga* ***burun burun*** *yure teru*
> 走っている女の子を見てごらん。胸が**ぶるんぶるん**揺れてる。

muchi muchi ★★★
むちむち
Well-fleshed and looking as if it might burst at any moment.

> **The best body shape is that of a chubby woman like muchi muchi.**
> *besutona taikei wa,* ***muchi muchi*** *shite iru pocchari shita joseida*
> ベストな体型は、むちむちしているぽっちゃりした女性だ。

puni puni ★★★
ぷにぷに
The feeling you get when you touch something soft.

Let me touch your *puni puni* tits. In return, you can touch my *puni puni* tummy.
*kimi no **puni puni** shita oppai o sawara sete. Okaeshi ni boku no **puni puni** shita onaka o sawatte ī yo*
君のぷにぷにしたおっぱいを触らせて.お返しに僕のぷにぷにしたおなかを触っていいよ。

momi momi ★★★
もみもみ
A cute way of describing the feeling of being squished (揉む [*momu*: squish]).

Can I squeeze yours a little like *momi momi*?
*kimi no mono o **momi momi** shite ī*
君のものをもみもみしていい?

torōn ★★
とろーん
Looks like it's about to melt. Also used when someone has a look of ecstasy on their face.

Your eyes are so glazed over, like *torōn*—are you feeling good?
*me ga **torōn** to shite irukedo, kimochiī no*
目がとろーんとしているけど、気持ちいいの?

I'm not aware of any other books besides this one that introduce erotic onomatopoeia. You're not allowed to make erotic onomatopoeia videos on YouTube. I once made a video titled "ムラムラ (*muramura*: horny)". It wasn't erotic at all; it was just a story about a misunderstanding between me and a friend, but I was stripped of the ability to monetize it just for talking about that episode. LOL.[5]

---

5 Were my words that erotic? You be the judge: https://youtu.be/TVfGZKK-uDY.

CHAPTER 9

ANGRY JAPANESE

MUKAMUKA NIHONGO

ムカムカ日本語

Just to be clear, there are no really bad swear words in Japanese. When you want to swear at someone, you express it through your voice, the way you say it, and your attitude. As you can often see in anime, when a cute girl says "バカ (*baka*: stupid)," it's very cute, and there are many men, including myself, who actually want to be told that. However, if a strong, scary guy says *baka* to you in a loud voice, it might really be scary. So, it would be a good idea to study how different people say things rather than just the words themselves.

I myself don't use many swear words—at least not aimed at people—because the moment I do, no matter how bad the other person is, I feel terrible. This may be a question of character. (Though it's very interesting I'm writing a book part of which is about saying such things!) In the next section I'm going to teach you some swear words, but I hope you won't use them very much.

·····Smacktalk

waruguchi

悪口

Die and go to hell ★★★

shine

死ね

Die right now ★★★

imasugu shine

今すぐ死ね

Hell ★★★

jigoku

地獄

Go to hell! ★

jigoku ni ochiro!

地獄に落ちろ!

loser ★★★

makeinu

負け犬

You're such a loser!

kono makeinu ga

この負け犬が!

Annoying ★★★

uzai

うざい

Don't talk to me, because you're annoying.

uzai kara hanashi kakete konai de

うざいから話しかけてこないで。

Piss me off ★★★
mukatuku
ムカつく

Your face pissed me off.
omae no kao ga mukatsuku
お前の顔がむかつく。

Suicide ★★
jisatsu
自殺

Don't commit suicide.
jisatsu shinai de
自殺しないで。

As a doctor, I would like to talk a little about suicide. Unfortunately, there are people who attempt suicide in every country, and the suicide rate is particularly high in Japan. There seem to be various factors behind this, such as the country's environment, the national character, and the economic situation, either of society as a whole or of the particular person.

When I was working in a hospital, I saw many people who had attempted suicide. With the development of medical care, many of them were saved, though in some cases, they were connected to IV tubes in a state of near brain-death and had to continue living a life of suffering for the rest of their lives.

People who attempt suicide are in a painful situation, but if talking to family or friends doesn't help, they should speak to a mental health counselor or doctor. In psychiatry, the feeling that you wish or for some reason "ought" to commit suicide is considered an illness. In fact, the desire to commit suicide is often caused by depression.

Even if you're feeling extremely depressed and it seems like there's no other way out but to die, this feeling is neither your fault nor a result of any fault of yours. It's most likely caused by a hormonal imbalance in your body that can be corrected. So, I know these situations can be really tough, but I want you to go and see a medical professional if you are having suicidal thoughts. That's a promise between you and me, okay? If you are in Japan, here is the Ministry of Health, Labor and Welfare's website with the phone numbers of suicide hotlines. If you need anything at all, definitely call them: www.mhlw.go.jp/stf/seisakunitsuite/bunya/hukushi_kaigo/seikatsuhogo/jisatsu/soudan_tel.html.

······Angry phrases

ikari no furēzu

怒りのフレーズ

Bad boys (delinquents) **are so lame, aren't they?** ★★★
***furyou** tte dasai yo na*
不良ってダサいよ?

He/she is such a liar. ★★★
*aitsu wa **usotsuki** da*
あいつは嘘つきだ。

He/she totally thinks he's the shit (i.e., a badass). ★★★
*aitsu **chōshi ni notteiru** yo ne*
あいつ調子にのっているよね。

He/she must think he/she is too cool for school. ★★
*aitsu wa jibun no koto o meccha **kakkō** ī to omottendaro*
あいつは自分のことをめっちゃ格好いいと思ってんだろ。

He/she is such an asshole. ★★★
*aitsu wa **kanji warui** kara*
あいつは感じわるいから。

Oh my god, he/she is so creepy. ★★★
aitsu wa hontō ni ***kimoi***
あいつは本当にキモイ。

He/she has been talking shit about me. ★★★
aitsu wa ore no ***warukuchi*** *o itteiru*
あいつは俺の悪口を言っている。

He/she always stands me up at the last minute. ★★★
aitsu wa itsumo ***dotakyan*** *suru*
あいつはいつもドタキャンする。

He/she is self-centered. ★★★
aitsu wa ***jikochū*** *da*
あいつは自己中だ。

He/she is no fun at all. ★★★
aitsu wa ***tsumannai*** *yatsu da*
あいつはつまんないヤツだ。

He/she is a total traitor. ★★★
aitsu wa ***uragirimono*** *da*
あいつは裏切り者だ。

He/she pisses me off. ★★★
aitsu ***atama ni kuru***
あいつ頭に来る。

Oh my god, I cannot stand him/her! ★★★
maji ***mukatsuku*** *aitsu*
マジむかつく、あいつ!

He/she really gets on my nerves. ★★★
aitsu maji ***uzai***
あいつ、マジうざい。

We'll never make up. ★★★
nakanaori *wa mō muri da na*
仲直りはもう無理だな。

I never want to see them again. ★★★
mō nido to ***aitakunai***
もう二度と会いたくない。

•••••Enemies
teki
敵

Sex predator ★★★
chikan
痴漢

A sex predator tried to feel me up on the subway.
chikatetsu de ***chikan*** *ni atte, watashi no mune o sawarō to shiteita no*
地下鉄で痴漢にあって、わたしの胸をさわろうとしていたの。

Stalker ★★★
sutōkā
ストーカー

So you were the stalker.
omae ga ***sutōkā*** *datta noka*
お前がストーカーだったのか。

Secretly taking photos ★★★
tousatsu
盗撮

Secretly taking photos is a crime.
tousatsu *wa hanzai desu*
盗撮は犯罪です

As a person of Japanese descent, I am very embarrassed by the fact that, though the risk of someone being a victim of a violent crime is considerably lower in Japan than in many other countries, voyeurism and groping tend to be more common here than elsewhere. I honestly don't understand the mentality of the people who do this, but it happens. I know people close to me who have been victims of groping on the train, so I think it's not uncommon. If you visit Japan, be aware of these dangers so you can avoid unpleasant experiences during your visit.

Cheapskate ★★★
kechi
ケチ

My old man is a stingy bastard.
uchi no oyaji wa dai no ***kechi*** *da*
うちの親父は大の**ケチ**だ。

Slowpoke ★★
guzu
グズ

I hate slowpokes.
watashi wa guzu wa kirai da yo
私はグズは嫌いだよ。

Boss ★★★
buchō
部長

My boss is a total fucking asshole.
uchi no ***buchō*** *wa maji mukatsuku*
うちの**部長**はマジむかつく。

Ex-boyfriend ★★★
motokare
元カレ

My ex-boyfriend was seriously evil.
atashi no ***motokare*** *wa hontō ni saiaku na yatsu datta*
あたしの**元カレ**は本当に最悪なヤツだった。

Ex-girlfriend ★★★
motokano
元カノ

My ex-girlfriend was a bitch.
*ore no **motokano** wa bicchi datta*
俺の**元カノ**はビッチだった。

Mother-in-law ★★★
giri no okāsan
義理のお母さん

My mother-in-law is the devil.
***giri no okāsan** wa onibaba da*
義理のお母さんは鬼婆だ。

……Snapping (losing your temper)
kireru
キレる

If step one of anger is getting pissed off, then step two is losing your temper, or snapping. The Japanese word for snapping, "切れる (*kireru*: be cut)," means exactly the same thing: The delicate thread suspending your overwrought composure has just snapped in half with an unbecoming twang.

He/she called me fat and I snapped. ★★★
*aitsu ni debu tte iwarete **kireta***
あいつにデブって言われて**キレた**。

He/she loses their shit really easily. ★★★
*aitsu wa sugu **kireru** mon*
あいつはすぐ**キレる**もん。

Don't snap at me! ★★★
***kireru na** yo*
キレるなよ!

Another word heard in this context is *gyaku gire* (逆ギレ), which literally means "snapping back"—such as when you get angry and scold someone who's late, and they get angry and say (they "snap back"), "There's no need to get so angry!" where the person is trying to avoid taking responsibility for their own mistake by becoming angry.

Snapping back at ★★★
gyaku gire
逆ギレ

When I got mad at my girlfriend she snapped back at me.
kanojo ni kirete mitara ***gyaku gire*** *sarechatta*
彼女にキレてみたら**逆ギレ**されちゃった。

Give a dirty look ★
gantsukeru
ガンつける

He/she gave me a dirty look.
aitsu ni ***gantsuke*** *rareta*
あいつに**ガンつけ**られた。

haul off and deck ★★
bunnaguru
ぶん殴る

I just wanna haul off and deck that motherfucker.
bunnagutte *yaritai*
ぶん殴ってやりたい。

•••••Fighting
kenka
けんか

There is a Japanese proverb, "口は災いの元 (*kuchi wa wazawai no moto*: Out of the mouth comes evil)." To avoid such evils, even when they are not at fault, Japanese people sometimes apologize to defuse a situation, following the philosophy that the best way to win a battle is to avoid it in the first place. Nevertheless, we will explore some fighting words below.

You suck. ★★★
omae saitei dana
お前最低だな。

Fuck off. ★★★
uzēndayo
うぜーんだよ。

What the fuck? ★★★
ahoka
アホか!?

Leave me the fuck alone. ★★★
shitsukoindayo
しつこいんだよ。

What did you just say!?! ★★★
nandato
なんだと?

You got a problem? ★
monku akka
文句あっか?

Bring it on! ★
kakatte koi
かかってこい!

Get out of my way. ★★★
doke
どけ。

Annoying ★★★
damarē urusē
うるせー

Shut up. ★★★
damare
だまれ。

Eat shit. ★
kusokurae
くそくらえ。

I hate you. ★★★
daikirai
大嫌い。

You're worthless. ★★★
tsukaenē yatsu dana
つかえねーやつだな。

••••••Stopping a fight
kenka o tomeru
けんかを止める

Keep a cool head. ★★
atama o hiyashitoke
頭を冷やしとけ。

Hey, calm down. ★★★
oi ***ochitsuke*** *yo*
おい、落ち着けよ。

Dude, don't lose your temper like that. ★★★
sonna ni ***kireru*** *na yo*
そんなにキレるなよ。

Take a **deep breath** or something. ★★★
shinkokyū *demo shiro*
深呼吸でもしろ。

You're all **worked up.** ★★★
kōfun *shisugi dayo*
興奮しすぎだよ。

Violence is bad. ★★★
bōryoku *wa damedayo*
暴力はだめだよ。

Peace is the best. ★★★
heiwa *ga ichiban sa*
平和が一番さ。

I'm a **pacifist.** ★★
watashi ***heiwa shugisha*** *nandesu*
私、平和主義者なんです。

Forget **about it,** man. ★★★
hottoke *yo*
ほっとけよ。

I have **nothing to do with this.** ★★★
kotchi ***kankei nē*** *yo*
こっち関係ねーよ。

Who really **cares?** ★★★
dōdemo *ījanē ka?*
どうでもいいじゃねーか?

Stop it. ★★★
yameroyo
やめろよ。

Whatever, man. ★★★
katte ni shiro
勝手にしろ。

••••••Cops ★

satsu

サツ

The cops showed up! Get outta here!
***satsu** ga kita! nigero!*
サツが来た！逃げろ！

Police ★★★
keisatsu
警察

Policeman ★★
omawarisan
お巡りさん

Run away! ★★★
nigero
逃げろ！

Oh, shit. ★★★
yabai
やばい。

It's a biker cop! ★
***shirobai** da*
白バイだ！

Hide the shit. ★
***yaku** o kakuse*
ヤクを隠せ。

I don't know anything. ★★★
***nani mo** shiranainda*
何も知らないんだ。

CHAPTER 10

LGBTQIA+ JAPANESE

LGBTQIA+ NIHONGO

LGBTQIA+ 日本語

Unfortunately, we have reached the final chapter on dirty Japanese. For our last chapter, let's learn some vocabulary that might be used in the LGBTQIA+ community. This community is very diverse, so we will just cover the most common terms for now.

•••••BL ★★★

bīeru

BL

BL (*bīeru*: BL) is a generic term for literary and video works and genres that feature male homosexual relationships. It stands for "boy's love."

> **To be honest, I like BL dramas.**
> *jitsuwa watashi, **bīeru** dorama ga suki nanda*
> 実は私、BLドラマが好きなんだ。

Yaoi ★★★
yaoi
やおい
Is an abbreviation for three phrases: "*yama nashi*" (no climax), "*ochi nashi*" (no punchline), and "*imi nashi*" (no meaning), combined to form the word "*Yaoi*." This is the general term for literary and video works and genres that mainly focus on male-male sexual love.

Top ★★★
seme
攻め
Is the person who inserts during a physical relationship between two men. It can also refer to the person who takes the lead mentally, even if there is no physical relationship. Also known as: タチ (*tachi*), 左 (*hidari*), and トップ (*toppu*).

Bottom ★★★
uke
受け
Is the person who is penetrated. The person who is submissive. Also known as: ネコ (*neko*), 右 (*migi*), and ボトム (*botomu*).

Versatile ★★
riba
リバ
Is a word that means that you can be top or bottom.

Heterosexual ★★★
noke
ノンケ
Is a term used by homosexuals to refer to heterosexuals. The word is a combination of the English word "no" and the Japanese word "気 (*ke*)" (meaning "signs," "moods," or "signs of homosexuals").

Fujoshi ★★★
fujoshi
腐女子
Literally, "rotten girl." Is a term for women who are obsessed with literary and video works featuring male-male romance and sex. The word "腐 (*fu*)" means "rotten."

Rotten Phoenix ★
fenikkusu
腐死鳥
Is a term used to refer to women with a lot of experience as *fujoshi*. The word, a coinage, is a play on the pronunciation of the original Japanese word for phoenix "不死鳥 (*fushityou*: Phoenix)." It is often used in a self-deprecating way as the ultimate pinnacle of *fujoshi*.

Fudanshi ★
futanari
腐男子
Is a term for a man who likes "boy's love" literary and video works in the same way as *fujoshi*. However, just because a man is a *fudanshi* does not mean he is a homosexual.

……Lesbians
rezu
レズ

In the case of lesbians, the terms "タチ (*tachi*: top) ★★★" and "ネコ (*neko*: bottom) ★★★" are more commonly used than the terms "攻め (*seme*: top)" and "受け (*uke*: bottom)" used in BL.

Completely top ★★
bari tati
バリタチ
Means completely top, never bottom or passive. The word "バリ (*bari*)" means "extremely," "completely," or "totally."

Totally bottom ★★
bari neko
バリネコ
Means completely bottom, never being a top and never initiating.

Lesbian ★★★
rezu
レズ

Lesbian ★★★
yuri
百合
Has a vague meaning depending on the person, but compared to the word "レズ (*rezu*: lesbian)," which is used as a frank expression of sexual orientation, the word *yuri* means a lighter form of female homosexuality. For some people, it is considered a romantic relationship that does not involve anything sexual at all.

Tomboy ★
jaritachi
ジャリタチ
Refers to a boyish, childish top. It is used in a slightly negative sense.

Top wearing feminine clothes ★
sukatachi
スカタチ
Is the top position during sexual intercourse, but it also refers to a lesbian who acts masculine but dresses and presents feminine.

A woman who acts like a man ★
danā
ダナー
Is a woman who likes to behave in a masculine way. The word comes from the Japanese word "旦那 (*danna*: husband)."

……Gay brothel
gei fūzoku
ゲイ風俗

A famous area in Japan where gay people gather is "新宿二丁目 (*shinjuku ni chou me*: Shinjuku 2-chome)." There are many LGBTQIA+ bars and sex establishments. There are two types of gay entertainment. Let's introduce them first.

Gay massage (ゲイマッサージ：*gei massāj*) is mainly, as the name suggests, about massage, and they provide a relaxing experience with hand jobs.

However, you are often not allowed to touch the other person. Make sure to check the rules. This is recommended for those who want to feel good in a relaxed and easy way. The going rate (in 2024) is around 5,000 to 10,000 yen ($32 to $64) for a 60-minute session.

Gay massage ★★★
gei massāji
ゲイマッサージ

Do you do hand jobs?
rifuresshu arimasu ka
リフレッシュありますか?
Literally, "Is there a refresh?," which is a reference to *rifuresshu* (リフレッシュ; refreshment), another name for service that includes a hand job.

Another type of gay sex establishment is 売り専 (*urisen*). This type of service allows you to have sex. Unlike female sex establishments, it is legal to have anal sex here, as Japanese law allows people to pay for anal sex. Basically, most of these establishments are on call, and they will be sent to your home or hotel. The general pattern is to meet up nearby and check in together.

Gay prostitute ★★★
urisen
売り専

A boy who works as 売り専 (urisen) ★★
bōi
ボーイ
Urisen is both a gay prostitute and a gay sex establishment.

Because there is no possibility of pregnancy, condoms are sometimes not used, but this does not stop the spread of HIV and other sexually transmitted diseases. Participants need to be careful about this.

•••••Lesbian brothel
rezu fūzoku
レズ風俗

Not all customers of female entertainment services are necessarily looking for physical pleasure, so in addition to the usual services, many people also take dating courses and sleeping together courses at these brothels.

For a fee, it is also possible to take videos. Of course, Surreptitious filming is prohibited. There're also other paid options such as vibrators, double-headed dildos, etc.

What was interesting for me during my research was レズビアン鑑賞コース (*rezubian kanshou kōsu*: the lesbian appreciation course). This is a course where you watch two women performing sexually in front of you. You can't participate yourself, but you can masturbate to it. Men can also book this course, since all you have to do is watch. However, the price is expensive as it is for two people. On the site I looked at, it was around 45,000 yen ($285) for 60 minutes.

The lesbian appreciation course ★
rezubian kanshou kōsu
レズビアン鑑賞コース

·····Pervert ★★★

hentai
変態

What is 変態 (*hentai*: a pervert)? If you search online for "hentai" in English-speaking countries, you'll find links to erotic manga, but in Japan when we use the word *hentai*, we refer to "sexual behavior different from the norm," or "abnormal sexual behavior."

However, it is difficult to clearly distinguish what is "normal" and what is "abnormal" in this world. In fact, in everyday life, the word "変態 (*hentai*)" is often used to refer to someone who is "thinking dirty thoughts." Even if it's not "abnormal sexual behavior," if you suddenly say to a woman, "I want to have sex with you," she might say, "この変態！(*kono hentai!*: You pervert!)."

If you watch a lot of anime, you may have seen women saying things like this. I tried to analyze why it is used slightly differently from its original meaning. Perhaps the person saying this means "I'm not a vulgar person who thinks dirty thoughts like you," and so says "pervert!" defensively, in response. In Japan in particular (and this is the case in many parts of the world), sexual behavior is often treated as something to be ashamed of, and sometimes as something vulgar. And women in Japan are educated to not be vulgar.

As human beings, we are creatures who control our instincts with reason, but we all have a considerable amount of sexual desire lying dormant within us, including such women, whether or not they are aware of it.

Japan is famous for its pornographic videos, and as a result, Japanese women are often viewed in a sexual light, but in reality, I don't think many Japanese women are that open about sex. Perhaps you have seen videos of interviews with Japanese women on YouTube, and you may have the impression there are many sexually active women in Japan. But this is an illusion. Such videos, showing the kind of Japanese women that are the ideal of many viewers, are distributed widely on YouTube. That's exactly what the YouTubers who created them want. I also have a YouTube channel, with 400,000 subscribers, so I understand that very well. But the videos I referred to above can create a false impression.

In any case, when you think about the definition of "pervert" again, you can come to the conclusion that "we are all perverts." Each person has their own unique obsessions, and because they like them more than the average person, they can seem to be "perverts." Considering that we are all perverts to some extent, we could redefine "pervert" as someone who goes beyond a certain range of behavior.

I know someone who put beads in his penis, got an infection, and had a high fever and nightmares. I thought he must have really regretted it, but he said, afterward, that he wanted to put in a few more. However we define "pervert," I think he could be called very "perverted."

There is, of course, a difference between "perversion" and "crime," and we must never, under any circumstances, do anything that is a crime. What is a crime changes depending on the era and country, but we need to live according to the rules (laws) of where we live. For example, if you tried to engage in prostitution in Japan just because you learned about it in this book, you would be arrested, probably be deported, and could even be banned from Japan.

So, let's all enjoy being "perverted," but always within the rules. We humans are all the same, regardless of gender or race, and we are all creatures with desires. Let's enjoy life within the rules, though without being overly restrictive.

POSTSCRIPT

ATOGAKI

あとがき

I hope you enjoyed reading this book and had fun learning your new vocabulary. If you use this book with sensitivity and good judgment, you could become popular—but if you don't, you could become a jerk. It's up to you.

I was chosen as the author of *Dirty Japanese, Second Edition*, and am very grateful to Ulysses Press for finding me among so many possible writers. When I first did a Zoom session with the publisher, she told me with a twinkle in her eye that I was the perfect author for this book. My YouTube content isn't very dirty, but I guess she had the ability to read my mind. At that moment, I must have looked like a hacker who had just been tracked down.

I worried that if I wrote this book, many women might hate me—but that if such a book could help a lot of men and women, it would be fine. Writing it was a fun opportunity to learn about a new world for me. I think doing creative projects like this book really suits me.

I have always loved creating interesting things. When I was little, I made a piece of art in art class using papier-mâché. It was a sushi roll with a tongue wrapped around it; it horrified my art teacher. When as a primary school student I had to do poetry homework, I loved tuna in sushi, and I had an inspiration when I saw my grandma lying down at home watching TV. "Grandma, your body is like tuna." I thought this phrase made a good poem, but my teacher and grandma got angry with me. After reading this book, you know why!

Even when I became a university student, my curiosity to do various interesting things didn't subside, and I wanted to try something new. At that time, everyone around me started using YouTube, and I was told that if I used YouTube, I could easily become famous and make money, but I thought that was a lie. However, I had a friend who had 10,000 YouTube subscribers, and I thought that it might be possible, so I started watching YouTube for the first time.

At the time, I had no money at all, so I spent the 100,000 yen that had been distributed to each member of the Japanese public because of the COVID epidemic and bought a camera. I started a YouTube channel, but at first, no one watched what I made. I watched videos on YouTube about how to be successful over and over again, and I did exactly what they said, but it was all a lie. At least for me, it didn't have any effect.

So I forgot about all the superficial techniques and concentrated only on making fun videos that would showcase my creativity. Until now, I had been paying more attention than necessary to image quality, audio, and other factors, deliberately making videos longer and making thumbnails prominent with YouTube's algorithm in mind. However, these are essentially unimportant. The most important thing really is to create videos that you would want to watch yourself. Even if the picture quality is poor or the audio is somewhat difficult to hear, if the content is interesting, people will watch it. But of course, my experiences on YouTube were not all successes.

I learned there were people who wanted to be able to speak Japanese through YouTube, so I tried to create an online Japanese school that specialized in conversation. However, although I was able to create very good content and it was well received, I didn't have much business knowledge, so it became hard to continue and I had to stop.

At the time, I was devastated by my own powerlessness, and I had spent all my money, so it was difficult to live from day to day. At the same time, I began to train as a resident doctor, so I took a break from YouTube and concentrated on my medical work.

Despite this break, Ulysses Press found me and offered me a job writing this book. In fact, the offer for this book has motivated me to get into YouTube and business again, for which I am truly grateful. In *Dirty Japanese, Second Edition*, I have not only defined "dirty Japanese" words, but I have also given examples to show how they're used. I have also tried to write about contemporary Japanese culture in as realistic a way as possible, with content that is not found on the internet. I hope that by using this book to understand the dirty side of Japan, your life will become richer!

ACKNOWLEDGMENTS

First, I would like to thank my Onomappu channel subscribers. Without each and every one of you, I would not have had this opportunity. I also want to thank アニャ(Ania) and ウカシ (Ukashi) for helping me get my YouTube started and for teaching me a lot about the challenges of learning Japanese as a second language. Next, I can't thank Joshua Sine enough for partnering with me on many various projects. He helped me a lot in making this book, giving me advice from a foreigner's point of view, and helping me with the English translation as well. Emerald O'Brien also helped me add a section about "affirmative consent," to make this book more educational. I would also like to thank all my friends. I will never forget the times we sat together in a family restaurant, seriously debating dirty phrases in the middle of the day. Finally, I can't thank everyone at Ulysses Press enough for allowing me the opportunity to produce this book. Thanks to them, I was given the freedom to create a book I am truly proud of—one that isn't "politically correct" but gives a real, raw peek into the Japanese words we use in situations that would never be included in any academic textbook. And last, I would also like to pay tribute to Matt Fargo, the author of the first edition of *Dirty Japanese*.

ABOUT THE AUTHOR

Hitoki is a native Japanese speaker with a passion for lifelong learning. In his journey to connect and support lifelong learners, Hitoki has also studied Chinese, English, and Spanish. Professionally, he's a doctor who mastered the art of learning while studying the human brain. His YouTube channel "Onomappu" demonstrates this with fun videos so interesting that viewers forget they're learning! This same technique is showcased in *Dirty Japanese, Second Edition*—a fun read containing real Japanese not taught in schools or textbooks.

Learn more about Hitoki and his future projects!

Follow him on YouTube and X (for enjoyable, entertaining content): Onomappu.

And on Instagram (for more active personal stories): Onomappu.

Join his mailing list for news about his next exciting projects: https://taplink.cc/hitoki.